Somewhere in the Middle

A Memoir About Healing

MELISSA TONI

PAGE PUBLISHING, INC.
Conneaut Lake, PA

First originally published by Page Publishing 2020

ISBN 978-1-64701-141-3 (pbk)
ISBN 978-1-64701-142-0 (digital)

Printed in the United States of America

To every person, place, and thing that has led
me to this moment. I am grateful.

Chapter One

It's October, but the leaves are still green. I push them out of the way as I stumble through the overgrown trail. I'm not sure where I'm headed or if I'm reading these markers correctly, but I continue on anyway.

"Root, dirt, stump, mushroom," I mutter to the ground. I'm trying to stay in the moment, but my mind is racing. The rocks in my backpack feel heavier today than they have all summer. I grip the shoulder straps and pull the backpack closer to my body. One of the rocks slips past the inner lining and begins thumping against my lower back. I'm too distracted to care.

"Beetle, grass, poison ivy, dog shit."

I haven't seen anyone else out in these woods, but I feel crowded. I rub my forehead, trying to ease the building tension and doubt. *Are these hikes really helping? Does it even matter if I carry these rocks at all?* I step over a cluster of roots and veer right. At this point, I have no idea where I am.

After a while, I come to a straightaway of pines, perpendicular to the path I'm on. I try to breathe in deep, slow and steady, the way my counselor always says, but my chest stops short. The sweet, spiced air tastes stale on my tongue. I scratch my arm, irritated by a crawling sensation, and turn left at the intersection. I'm hoping to loop back to the main trail, but I can't know for sure. All I know is I have to keep moving. The loose rock in my backpack and my thoughts continue to pound.

I hurry down the wide pine-bedded path, propelled now only by determination. I've given up counting objects. I let my eyes glaze over, and my thoughts swell against my skull. The static increases like a million buzzing insects between my ears. I look to the thin strip of sky above me for relief, but there are only heavy gray clouds. *Has this all been a waste of time?* I don't know what I believe anymore. I'm starting to think I was wrong.

The wall of trees to my right opens up, and suddenly, I find myself standing in front of a small beach on the edge of a dark wakeless lake. I walk out to the stone wall bordering the few feet of sand and sit with my bloated backpack strapped on. The noise inside my head settles a bit but still hums as I stare out at the vast space. In the middle of the water, something grabs my attention. I squint, hating what I see.

Without thinking, I stand up and unclip my backpack, letting the weight drop to my feet. I take off my baseball hat and pull my hair loose from the elastic, ripping my hoodie off over my head. My shirt, my pants, my underwear and socks—they all come off swiftly. I leave everything in a pile, discarded on the stone wall, and then I walk to the edge of the lake, ignoring the hand beckoning from the deep. I ease myself into the water, watching the cool, wavering line creep up my waist, and then I lie down with my head held just above the surface. As I float there, the clouds of muck clear, revealing my naked body submerged in tints of brown and rust. I hardly recognize myself. I've stared at my body a million times in the mirror—poked, picked, scratched, and scrutinized every night before bed for as long as I can remember—but underneath the dark surface, I am foreign. Little fish begin to gather, curious and hungry.

All at once, I cup my hands over my ears, blocking out the external sound, and exhale to sink beneath the surface of the water. At the bottom of the lake, all feelings and thoughts finally drown out. The murkiness settles over me as the fish nibble gently on my skin.

Chapter Two

I rub my eyes, disturbed by the fluorescent lights. The sky outside looks dark, or maybe the window is tinted. I shift in my seat and graze the cold metal armrests, folding my arms against my body. My psychiatrist is busy reading over my file. With her eyes distracted, I uncross my arms and let my hands lie stiff on my lap. My fingers gravitate toward each other and begin to pick, searching for flakes of skin. I wish I knew how to sit still.

"All right, let's see here, let's see. So you're still taking the Latuda at night. Correct? And you were experiencing night sweats, but last time I saw you, we realized that was a temporary symptom. How has your sleeping been lately?"

"Better. I mean…all I ever want to do is sleep."

She jots something down as I gaze out the window. The glass is definitely tinted. Strange how I've never noticed before.

"What about your drinking? Did you and your sister go to that music festival yet?"

"We did." I smile slightly. "We actually just came back yesterday."

She looks up.

"And how did that go?"

"Good. Better than I anticipated."

"Did you drink?"

I bite my nail. I had to know this question was coming. "Yeah, but we didn't go overboard. Neither of us blacked out."

She puts her pen down and leans back in her swivel chair to face me. I try my best to wait out her stare, but my eyes glaze over. I look down, aware that she picks up on everything.

"Blacking out isn't normal. You shouldn't even be drinking on these pills."

"I know." I look to my hand. A hangnail lifts. I try to saw it off with the edge of my nail, but the flap of skin resists like rubber. I roll it back and forth, and then tear it off. My finger starts to bleed.

"What about your counselor? Have you brought up your drinking issue with her yet?"

"No." I draw my sleeves down to conceal my hands. "I don't have a problem with drinking. That's my sister's issue."

"What about your eating?" She doesn't miss a beat. "Have you talked to your counselor about that?"

I shake my head and turn away. I don't need to see her face to know what she's thinking. Last time I saw my counselor, we didn't talk at all. We spent the hour doing Reiki. Everything she and I do together makes sense in the moment, but in the harsh light of this office, I question everything. I never looked forward to counseling before this year. I thought my enthusiasm for her unique approach was a good thing, but maybe I'm just naive.

"You need to talk to someone. That's why you have a counselor."

"I know." I want to say more, but the words fizzle out before they reach my throat. She returns to my file.

"How about your period? Is your cycle back to normal?"

My upper lip twitches. "Yes."

"Good. I knew the birth control would sort that out."

She closes my file and leaves the room to grab my pills. We have a routine. Somewhere down the hall, locked in a closet, she keeps a supply of free samples. Her shoes clap loudly down the linoleum floor. She returns fast and hands me several packs—enough to get me through the next month. I don't know what I'll do the day she runs out.

"Did you ever take a look at that magazine I gave to you?" She sits down to complete my checkout sheet.

"What magazine?" I don't know why I ask. I don't think I'll ever forget the front cover.

"The one I gave to you when we first met." She rips off the top sheet to hand to me. "You need to start taking your condition seriously. I suggest you do some research."

I take the paper and tuck it inside my purse along with my pills, and then I get up to leave. As I reach the door, I hesitate. Fifteen minutes is not enough time. It never is. I wish I could explain my side of the story, but she's already busy reading the next file. I walk out. She doesn't notice.

Inside my car, I roll up the windows and lock the doors. My mom says it smells like wet dog in here, but I guess after all these years of pet sitting, I've gotten used to it. Out of habit, I pull down my rearview mirror to check my face. I can't start up my car until I do. I move in close to examine the details, and then I pull away, repeating this several times. I sigh and shove the mirror back into place. I drive out of the parking lot before the stillness in the air takes over.

As I drive, I don't look around. My eyes stay fixed on the road in front of me. I keep my music turned up and my speed steady, reluctant to slow down but afraid to return home. My apartment feels different this year. The whole town of Newport feels different too. I wish I could blame someone or something for what happened, but I know everything that went wrong last August was because of me.

When I open my front door, my cat greets me. I bend down to pet her, and then I move into the kitchen to assemble my dinner. Lined evenly across the two bottom shelves of the refrigerator are seven salad kits and seven individually-packaged breasts of precooked chicken. I take out one of each and carefully lay the lettuce on a plate first, followed by the toppings, dressing, and chicken. I carry my salad and a glass of water into the living room, and then I sit on the floor in front of my coffee table to turn on the TV. The noise fills the room, but I don't listen. I could care less about the show. The volume stays on as a distraction. Once I'm finished with my salad, I return to the kitchen to clean up and review my whiteboard. I read over my list of goals even though I know them by heart, and then I add the final checkmark for the day next to "eat healthy." I stare for a moment, trying to feel satisfied, but nothing comes. I grab the eraser from the top of the board and carefully remove the checkmarks, ready to start the list all over again tomorrow.

My cat follows me into bed and nestles beside me as I reach for my pills. Down the far end of the shelf, there is a third bottle. I haven't opened it yet, but the thought often crosses my mind. The cap is coated with a thin layer of dust, and the position of the bottle hasn't changed since I brought it home and placed it there months ago.

Take one only if you absolutely need to.

My psychiatrist's words float through the air like they do every night. I leave the bottle and turn away. I know I can sleep through tonight.

Just before turning off the light, I bend over the side of my bed to dig underneath the stray papers and half-read books. At the very bottom, underneath the cat hair and crumbs, I find what I'm looking for. I brush off the top page and lay the magazine on my bed. The cover still makes me cringe. I shove the magazine back under my bed, gathering the books and paper and anything else in my reach to pile on top. I shut off the light and close my eyes, but the image remains. Through the dark, I can still see the man on the front cover, riding his miniature bike like a clown in a circus ring. The giant rocket strapped to his back is meant to be symbolic, and the exaggerated openmouthed expression on his face is meant to be amusing, but I don't find any of it clever or funny. It all makes me angry.

Chapter Three

I pull up to my apartment to wait for my mom. The clock says noon—exactly when I told her to meet me here, but she doesn't seem to understand time. *Deep breaths.* I have two dogs in my car and two waiting for me at the next house, but I'm trying not to think about that. I turn off the engine and lean back against the headrest. *What could possibly be taking her so long?* I force my jaw open to unhinge the tension. The left side pops. I never should have left her a key. I never should have let her quit her job and agreed to these weekly visits. I need to be grateful, but I can't be late.

The storm door creaks open as my mom steps out. She smiles and waves from the porch. I breathe in and wave back.

"Hello!"

Her voice sings. She holds the railing as her open-toed shoes clop carefully down the stairs. I squeeze my cheeks together, wanting to smile, but her flowery blouse and tight white jeans make me cringe. I start up the car and grip the steering wheel. She opens the door to brush off the passenger seat.

"Ooh, so much dog hair. I don't know how you can—oh! I didn't even see the dogs in the back! How adorable! What are these guys called again?"

"Puggles." My thumb taps the steering wheel. "They're a mixture between a pug and a beagle."

"That's right! So cute."

She reaches behind the seat to pet them. I lift the top of the center console to prevent one from jumping forward.

"Hey, Mom, I hate to be a pain, but we've gotta get going."

"Oh yes, of course!" She pulls her hand back and steps into the car. I start to drive as soon as she shuts the door.

"Sorry I took so long in your apartment. I had some groceries that needed to go in your fridge."

My stomach twists—nausea mixed with guilt and hunger.

"Mom, you didn't have to do that. I can buy my own groceries."

"Please, it's my pleasure! You know I love taking care of my baby."

I look out the window. At the stop sign, I scratch my neck and linger, taking a breath before glimpsing the traffic on my mom's side. I lean toward the door as we turn right.

"And I didn't buy any treats this time because I know you're trying to be good. Neither of us need that stuff in the house. It's too tempting."

I clear my throat and swallow the phlegm. "Thank you, but seriously, I don't need help with groceries." The sickness churns. "I really appreciate it, though. Everything you do. Thank you. I'm sorry."

"Don't be sorry. That's what I'm here for."

I merge onto Bellevue to join the line of cars. Traffic creeps slow as the river of silence opens between me and my mom. The current flows both ways—it has ever since the hospital. I look outside to the crowded sidewalks. Deep in my gut, bubbles begin to rise, but my mom talks over.

"So my week was busy. I had book club with my friends Wednesday, and dinner with Denise Thursday."

"Uh-huh." I follow the car in front closely.

"And this morning, I went to the gym of course, and then did my own grocery shopping. Your father has been *obsessed* with those nut bars. I can't keep enough in the house! And you know your sister, she's trying to be good too. Nut bars are the only dessert-like thing I'll keep in the house."

The light turns yellow. I slip through.

"And let's see, what else is new. Oh! I bought some new stuff for the house. Just a few paintings and knickknacks. Your father says we're running out of wall space, but I keep finding places to squeeze things in."

"Mhm." I turn right and head down the hill to the next house on my schedule. I park in the driveway and get out.

"Is this our next stop?"

"Yes. I'll be right back."

"Okay. Are we walking the puggles here or…?"

"Two seconds. I'll be back."

I shut the door and go around the side of the house. Once inside, I breathe. The owners aren't home—it's just me and the dogs. I sink to the floor as the little terriers yip and paw at my sides. I don't mind the scratches. Animals have always made sense to me—it's humans I don't understand. My body melts down as their tiny paws brush my thighs and their wet noses print my skin. My head feels heavy. I wish I could lie down and stay here for a while.

I take a deep breath before standing up to grab the harnesses. The dogs slip willingly in and prance beside me as we head outside, around to the car. My mom steps out. The terriers bark.

"Hi, guys! You remember me." She leans down to pet them, stiffening as they bark again.

"They remember. They do this to everybody." I scoop the male up to bring him to a safer height. He sniffs my mom's hand while the female sniffs her shoes. I place the terrier back down, and they both stand quietly. "They just need to know they're safe. Now they're okay."

I open the door and slide up the seat. The puggles jump out fast, but I hold their leashes tight in my right hand, leaving space between the two pairs of dogs. My mom reaches out.

"Let me help. I can walk someone."

I look to each gripped hand. I can't tell her it would be easier if she let me walk them. I can't remind her that I've been doing this on my own for nearly five years. I hand her the terriers as I calculate a new route. We're going to need to avoid most dogs. The terriers get aggressive around dogs they don't know, but I can't give my mom the puggles because they pull too hard. I lock my car and check the handle several times before leading my mom and the dogs up the hill.

"Ooh, are we going to Bellevue? I love walking by the mansions. I feel like a tourist!"

Her delight sours my intestines. I tighten my abdomen, resenting the feeling, wishing I could be a loving daughter. "Yeah. Good idea, Mom."

Exhaust fills the air as we near the traffic on Spring Street. At the intersection, a driver waves me on, but when I look behind, my mom is too far away. She's standing near a bush, stopped to let the male terrier pee. The leg goes down, but the dogs continue to sniff. I stare at the slack in the leash, the watch on my wrist, the gentle obliviousness on my mom's face.

"Mom, come on. People are waiting."

"Sorry! Here we come."

She tugs too lightly. The slack lifts, but the leashes don't pull. I wave the car on and rub my head. *Relax. Today is going to be a good day. Don't lose control.* As I wait for her to catch up, I try to think of something normal to say.

"How was Orlando?"

"Oh, it was great! Your father and I had such a wonderful time. He loves that I'm free now to join him on those trips." She follows me across the street. On the other side, I slow my pace.

"Good, Mom. I'm glad that's working out."

"It is! They're fun for me, of course, and your father loves the company. He calls me his little business trip buddy."

She smiles, eyes squinted in an unnatural way. I look down at the dogs. The puggles strain against their collars. I walk a little faster as my mom continues.

"And we were so lucky—perfect weather the whole time! Huge pool, amazing meals. We found some really good restaurants. Ooh, speaking of, where do you want to get dinner later?"

My stomach gurgles. I haven't eaten yet today.

"Um, I don't know. Wherever you want."

"Hmm, I'll have to think about it. I'm always in the mood for seafood…"

She stops again to let the terriers pee. I wait as my own dogs do the same, but after several more interruptions, I can't deny the tension in my face. Fifteen minutes have passed, and we still haven't reached Bellevue. On my own, the dogs and I would have made it there in five.

"Ooh, you know, I think I want a lobster roll later. I know I say that every time I come here, but I can't help it. It's Newport!"

"Sure, that sounds good, but can we keep moving? You don't have to let the dogs sniff everything."

The heat in my words singes the air. A group of people stare and step off the sidewalk to pass widely around. I look down. They were smiling before they neared me.

"Sorry! We'll keep up."

"No, Mom. I'm sorry. It's okay."

"Don't apologize! I get it. I'm being slow."

I turn away to close my eyes. Her words sting, but I clench and draw back the tears. I have to be stable.

"Oh, your sister told me all about the music festival! Sounds like you two had a great time."

I swallow. "We did. We had a lot of fun."

"That makes me so happy. I love when you two get along. You're both such smart, wonderful girls."

I turn away. The air is thin and tender. My lungs shake.

"Your sister seems so happy too. She really likes that guy. George? John? I can never remember his name."

"Creg."

"Creg! That's it. Yeah, can you believe how much she likes him? I've never seen her so excited about a guy before."

"Yeah, me neither."

"And they've only known each other for a few weeks. He must really be something."

A car beeps along Bellevue. I jump at the horn. My mom smiles.

"Wow, look at all the traffic! I forgot how busy this town gets in the summer."

A man stares from the open window of his car. I look down at the gravel. My mom continues to talk, but my ears can't filter through the sound. The idling engines and fumes pollute the air. The clash of radios and heated laughter distort in my mind. I close my eyes and breathe in slow, but the static doesn't clear.

You lost your mind. Everybody knows you lost your mind.

I squeeze my eyelids together—pressure to block out the sound. I look to my mom. She's still talking. I want to interrupt, but I know she won't understand. She says I'm paranoid. Maybe I am. I look to the sky, my dogs, the houses around me. Her voice returns.

"Look at that adorable front porch! I love the blue door."

I scratch my scalp. "Uh-huh."

"That's the color I wanted to paint our door, but I like the shade we ended up choosing. Turquoise has always been my favorite color."

"Mm, yeah."

"Oh! Your father and I took the kayaks out the other day. We had such a good time. You wouldn't believe all the birds we saw…"

I look at my watch. Time is moving slow. Pair after pair of eyes drift by. They all seem to know. Beneath my feet, the gravel shifts as a headache builds and cracks against my skull. I turn to my mom, pleading for her to notice, begging for her to stop talking and see, but her petty words persist. Underneath a bush, one of my puggles pulls. I want to join him and crawl beneath the leaves. I don't want to smile and nod and pretend anymore, but I can't go inward either. I peek up as a group of people steer around. Their faces, their eyes—they all blur and twirl like the background on a teacup ride. The tears start to form. My mom thinks we're moving forward, but all we're really doing is spinning.

"You'll never guess what I made for dinner the other night! It was actually your sister's suggestion—"

The cork pops. I explode.

"Jesus Christ, Mom, do you ever stop talking?" A shock wave paralyzes the scene. "Can't you see that I don't care about this shit? I *can't* care about this shit. I can't care about anything!"

I shield my face as the anger turns to tears. They burst out uncontrollably. I can hear the traffic creeping slow—curious eyes, sinister eyes drawn to the pain.

The dog walker's losing it again. We knew she would.

I bang my fist against my head. The internal judge laughs and grows louder. He knows the formula: the harder I fight, the crazier I look.

"Honey, please stop. What's wrong?"

My mom's softness doubles the tears. I take the next turn to lead her away from the busy street. I don't want to drag her into this. I don't want her to feel the way I feel. I hide around a wall of hedges on the edge of an empty driveway and wait for her to be hidden too.

"I want to care. Believe me, I want to care, but I can't. I pretend and pretend, but I'm not okay."

"But you've been doing so well." Her sweetness is close. "Every time I see you, you seem to be doing more. You're always working on a goal."

She rests her hand on my back, but the touch is too light. I shake away her ginger fingers, furious she can't use both arms and consume me like my dad.

"But that's the problem! I *can't* stop working on goals. As soon as I stop, everything comes crumbling down."

Her rejected touch retreats to her face—delicate nerves tap over her upper lip. I can't look at her fingers, but she can't look me in the eye. We both turn away, afraid for different reasons, struggling for similar words. I never should have lost control. I never should have let myself burst open like this.

"I'm sorry, Mom. I overreacted. I really am fine. I just had a moment of weakness."

She doesn't respond, so I look up. Her splayed fingers no longer tap. They wither and lock together—a hard ball covering her lips.

"Mom, it's okay."

I hug her tight, but she's stuck—frozen. She feels so small. *Why do I always have to ruin things?* I inch my arms further around, missing the mom I had a few seconds ago. I try not to think about the groceries or the hour-and-a-half-long drive she took to get here. I try not to think about her cheerful, unaware face. Or maybe she's too aware.

"Let's finish walking the dogs, and then we can head back to my apartment." I squeeze her once more and then pull away. "You can use my shower if you want, and then we can go get those lobster rolls."

She nods, eyes still averted. Slowly, she follows me back onto the street as a plastic bag drifts by. Down on Lower Thames, the breeze picks up, carried by window-shoppers and well-dressed tourists eager to eat. I turn around to scoop up the female terrier as a dog on a leash passes by. She barks and writhes in my arms, breaking the stagnant silence between me and my mom.

"Salt Bar would be fun. I love their outdoor seating."

I smile at her suggestion even though underneath I'm incredibly sad.

"Sounds good, Mom."

We head back to the terriers' house to drop them off and continue our day as if the last five minutes never happened.

Chapter Four

Through the cracks in my blinds, an orange glow seeps in. My cat is awake, curled up next to me, staring. I turn over and look at the clock: 5:20 a.m. I'm never up this early. At least I haven't been in a long time. I flip over and nestle closer to my cat, tucking my body around her in a crescent shape. The warm light coats and glistens through her field of fur. I run my fingers down the back of her neck, over the hills of soft sparkling black. I can still feel the dream. I bunch closer to the rolls of comforter, squeezing in the sleepy scent. A delightful foam ripples through the fluff as cotton fills my ears. I smile and close my eyes, seeping into wherever I had been. Sleep returns gently, but too soon, my alarm snaps me back. My cat springs from the bed as I reach down to shut off the sound. I moan and rub my eyes. The shades are a dull pale white. The memory of the dream lingers, but the afterglow has disappeared.

In the kitchen, my cat waits by her bowl. She knows the routine. I pour out her dry food and crack open a can. She eats immediately. I move to the counter to turn on the espresso machine. The button is hidden in the back, but my hand knows the location well. I open the fridge and pull out the espresso. The almond milk, the berries, they come out next. The coffee streams as I move to the cabinets, taking out the oatmeal and walnuts fast, aware of the filling cups keeping time. I pop the bowl of oats in the microwave, returning to the espresso machine to turn off the brew. The microwave beeps, so I fetch the bowl. I place my breakfast down at the table for two, where everything has its place. I lean my phone up against the iced espresso and press play. The *Ted Talk* loads as my spoon hovers. I can't eat until the video starts.

As the loading wheel spins, I look to the whiteboard on my fridge. *How long has the list been there? How long has it been since the bullets were erased?* I look back at the frozen video and the steaming bowl between. The oats are sunken. I drown them every morning with water to the rim, filling my stomach with liquid before consuming any calories. I do this twice, returning to the sink to drown the oats a second time. The wheel on the screen disappears, and the picture finally moves. My spoon drops down to begin the process as I follow along with the video, but the speaker on stage talks too slow. Too many pauses. I ex out and click another video randomly, but the next speaker is the same. Slurping loud and eating fast, I keep my eyes submerged in the bowl.

After breakfast, my cat trots in front of me to the bedroom. Her belly swings as she jumps up on the bed. I pull open the drawer to dig out my clothes. My shorts don't fit. Everything is too tight. I drift to the mirror and lift up my shirt, belly bloated, round with the liquid weight. My cat watches from her side, eyes squinted, body laid out and drooping over the comforter. I wish I could stay inside. I wish I could be like her. The mirror calls me back. I have no choice but to obey. I suck in and squeeze. I pinch, and I poke. Still, I know none of these rituals have any effect. I do them every day, but nothing can change the fact that I've gained twenty pounds.

Secretly in the car before dog walking, I stretch out my clothes. *The pills, the pills*, the psychiatrist in my head blames, but I know my weight issues began long before. I start the engine and turn the wheel as my car drifts mindlessly along. I turn on the wiper and spray, but the windshield never looks clean. I pull down my sleeve to smudge away the fog from inside. I only need a small spot to see. I make my way all over town, down the list in my planner, tracking every move through a shaky finger. As my day continues, the clear spot on my windshield starts to spread.

I pull up to my third stop—a three-story house a block up from Broadway. I park on the street and jog up the stairs to the second floor. Lucy, the Staffordshire terrier, waits inside. I grab the leash and collar from the wall hook and bend down to click the buckle around her neck. I check my watch and open the door, leading her to the edge of the stairs, but she resists.

"Come on, Lucy." I pull without looking. She should know the routine. I don't know why she's gotten so stubborn lately. I pull again, but this time, I turn around. Her eyes are big, surprised and a little sad. My tight grip on the leash loosens, but her head remains low. *How long has it been since I looked her in the eye? How long has it been since I looked any of my dogs in the eye?*

Carefully, she leans closer to smell my hand. Time slows as her wet nose dabs and nuzzles under my palm, running my touch over her wide forehead. I smile. A smooth mountain. Her gentle strength calms me.

I sit beside her on the top step to breathe and lean in. Time passes silently on my wrist, but I don't want to look. I don't want to care. Lucy licks my cheek, and through her laps of love, an overwhelming realization seeps in: I've forgotten who I am. I wrap my arms around her to cling to the moment and hold back the tears. These dogs aren't time-contingent tasks. That's not how I started this business. Five years ago when I had nothing—no hope, no money, no direction or place—the animals were the only thing that made sense. They brought me back—they showed me the way. *Why wouldn't they be able to show me again?*

I lean back to gaze at her sweet face.

"Do you want to do something different today?"

Her tail wags, thumping the ground. No time is lost. Lucy understands.

She walks beside me out to the car. I open the door, and she leaps in. As I walk to the driver's side, I look down the hill to Broadway where all the noise and chaos begins. My next two dogs live around here too, but they can wait. Lucy and I need to escape this busy street.

We drive around randomly, taking turns that appeal for unknown reasons. Eventually, we come to a dead-end street where the reservoir peeks through the trees. I unfasten the watch from my wrist, closing it up in the glove compartment. Lucy's front paws patter up and down on the seat, her ears perked, ready to jump outside. I let her out. She pulls, nails scratching at the pavement.

"Whoa! Where'd this Lucy come from?" I laugh. Her nose sniffs frantically, leading us both off the road and onto the grass. I could reel her in. I probably shouldn't let her pull, but I haven't seen her this excited in almost a year. She's seven, but in these tufts of emerald and untamed scents, she's filled with a puppylike energy.

As she soaks in the ground below, I look up to the trees, noticing the delicate blossoms of green. *When did they bloom?* Everyone says we had such a cold February, but I barely remember. The leaves withered and fell last fall, and the branches collected snow all winter, but I saw nothing. A branch hangs low to greet me as I near. I bend the arm down to look closer at the feathery leaves. The newborn skin is soft against my lips, so smooth it almost feels wet. I kiss the leaf. I don't know why, but I do, and then gently, I ease the branch back up above my head.

Lucy and I continue up the hill. At the top, my pace slows. As Lucy stops to investigate something on the ground, a light breeze swirls around, lifting my brow and widening my eyes. The light reflecting off the trees increases and pours in as a headache I hadn't been aware of disintegrates into a million flaky pieces up into the air. *What's happening?* There's no time to think. My chest opens up as a soft honeycomb glow radiates all over my skin. I can't see it, but I can feel it. I look up to the sky—blue, vast, and cloudless. Suddenly, a waterfall floods over me. The invisible liquid saturates my mind, awakening my senses. All I can do is stand as the rush of ideas washes over me. The river dries up, and the trickling stops. The sky closes back up, and my skull does the same. I breathe in and look around. Lucy is still sniffing. She didn't notice a thing. I rub my arm against the grain. The blond hairs are standing, reaching out to touch the delicate wind. The subtle sensation surprises me. I feel light and joyful, like a child.

"Lucy!"

She looks up, a blade of grass between her lips.

"I finally know what I want to do—what I *need* to do!"

She cocks her head and squints her eyes. She seems confused by my excitement. I laugh because I would be confused too by such a sudden change.

"Don't worry, I'm not losing it. I can't be. I'm still taking my pills…"

She stares a few seconds longer and then goes back to chewing grass. I squat down and kiss the top of her big, warm head. I wish I could kiss everyone right now. I haven't felt this alive since last summer.

We finish our walk and return to her house, but even without Lucy and away from the miraculous place, I carry the energy. I refill my water bottle at the next house and then fill it again two stops later. By the end of my day, I'm out of water. I finish the last drop as I cross out my final walk. My planner says I should go to the gym next—it's one of my daily goals—but I scribble it out and cross off the day, tossing my planner to the floor. I have bigger plans now. I drive out of Newport to the far end of Middletown. Soft wings flutter up my chest and powder my cheeks as I pull into the complex parking lot. I haven't been to a craft store in years. Until today, I haven't had a reason.

I shut the car door and hurry inside. My pace is fast—stride long and determined even though I have no idea where I'm going. I search up and down the different sections, reading the signs and slowing as I reach the back of the store. I pivot and breathe in. The idea is clear in my mind, but now that I'm here, I'm starting to doubt they have what I'm looking for. I move up to the front along the middle aisle, checking the bins and display cases in between. On a metal rack marked "clearance," I finally see it: four kits—three exactly the same, all precisely what I had in mind. I take one of each and walk away, returning fast to grab the other two. I dump the armful of boxes onto the nearest register and smile at the cashier. He glances down at my purchase. Heart pounding, I continue to smile.

"Are these all you have?"

He stares dully and nods.

"Okay, that's fine. This should be enough."

He rings up the boxes, glancing up between barcodes. I look away. I don't need to see his reaction. I don't need to feel his judgment or concern. He hands me the receipt, and I grab it fast to return home. I burst inside. Before dinner, before my shower, before stepping more than ten feet into my living room, I plop down on the floor and open one of the kits. My cat joins me and sits beside as I begin to paint my first rock.

Chapter Five

The doorbell rings. I turn down the music and finish the last of my beer before hurrying down the stairs. My arms fling open. Steve looks surprised.

"Hello!"

I pull him inside, stumbling as I lead him up to the second floor. He sits on the edge of the couch. I gravitate to the fridge.

"Want anything? I have vodka, beer, tequila, we could smoke…"

"Uh…sure. I'll have a beer."

The rhythm from the speaker melts across the living room and into the kitchen. I sing and sway as I take out the last beer and open the vodka. Behind the freezer door, I chug straight from the handle. The liquid burns, poisonous fumes rise up my throat, but I don't gag. I cap the bottle and close the freezer door, hiding it back inside.

"Here you g—"

The corner of the coffee table bangs against my knee. I laugh as I fall forward, one hand on the couch. Steve takes the beer and eases me down.

"Are you okay?"

"Yeah. I'm fine."

His hand is soft on my shoulder, his mouth too small and flat. I push off the cushion to open a window and feel the breeze. The heavy, intoxicated warmth swirls with the cool night air. My arms lift and dance in the contrast, the two swirling oppositions. Like oil and water, they stir together, but they never mix.

"How much have you had? You didn't sound drunk on the phone…"

"Don't be a fart! I'm just having fun."

I grab the remote to turn on the TV and put on a music video. Steve takes the speaker from the table to shut off the clashing sound.

"I know, but you seemed sober twenty minutes ago."

"Shh. Relax. Here, put on whatever video you want."

He takes the remote and sips his beer. "What do you feel like listening to?"

"Whatever *you* want, clown! You know how this works. We take turns."

He smiles and leans back. I knew he would. The music stops as he exits out the video to search for a new one. The floor tilts to the left as I stand watching the silent screen. He lights over the different squares but takes too long to choose. I wobble left but catch myself and disappear to the back room.

"So what's this big idea you wanted to tell me?"

His voice beams, the way it used to, the way I need it to. I straighten away from the dark corner of my bedroom and hurry around the other side to gather my rocks. A few slip out from under my arm and bounce on the bed. I place them on top and dump the pile in front of him on the floor. He laughs as I sit and spread them all around.

"Here it is! I'm so excited. I just finished step one last night. All I've been doing lately is painting rocks."

"I can see that!"

A guitar riff blasts in behind me. I turn around and squint to read the artist. I don't recognize the name. I bob my head to the beat and smile. Steve perks up.

"I thought you might like them!"

The beat skips as I cringe. I look down to refrain from his eyes. I fiddle with the rocks as I wait for the drums and baseline to return.

"So what do you mean by 'step one'? I'm so intrigued!"

I bob back in.

"Yes! Okay. So basically I…well, no. Where do I want to start? Ah, I get so excited every time I think about my plan!"

I spring from the floor and join him on the couch. His cheeks fill with a transmitted delight as I scoot closer.

"Phew! Okay, so here's where I want to begin. The other day, while dog walking, I had an epiphany. I know it sounds crazy, but I was just strolling along when suddenly this waterfall of ideas came over me. Not a real waterfall—I call it that because the whole plan came in fast, in a stream, but whatever. It doesn't matter. Point is, I feel like I have purpose again! I don't feel numb and dead anymore."

His smile twitches and falls down. "You felt numb and dead this whole time?"

I reach for his hand. "Well, no...you know what I mean." I cup his limp grip between mine and squeeze. The warmth pulses out my palms as his fingers absorb and curl around. My gaze drops down. "I don't know. I could be manic right now. Sorry I was talking so fast."

"No, no, you're fine! Honestly, this is kind of nice for a change." He takes both my hands. "Usually, I'm the one doing all the talking."

I laugh because it's true. He sips his beer.

"Okay, so continue with your plan. The suspense is killing me!"

Before he places the bottle down, I swipe it from him and drink. The fizz relaxes open my lips as a tiny trickle escapes and runs down my chin. I wipe it fast, but Steve's eyes are too sharp. He laughs, but in the sudden haze of remembered vodka, I don't mind that he sees. I want him to see everything.

"My plan..." My tongue is fat. The words slur. "Is to finally heal. Not the bullshit, cover-up, pill-popping crap heal but *really* heal."

"Okay. I gotta hear this."

My voice is far away. It disappears out into the foggy air. "All these painted rocks you see before your very eyes are *not* child's play." My finger pops up for emphasis but immediately falls back down. "Each one represents a burden I've been carrying around since I was a kid."

"Do you want to lie down?"

"No!" I sit up straight. "I got this. I'm going to tell you. Mmm." My head wobbles as my eyes try to focus on Steve. He looks so big and warm, so cozy and near. I crawl over and sit on his lap. He laughs as I wrap my legs around.

"And what are you planning to do with these rocks?"

"Shhhh. It doesn't matter."

I grab his face and melt into his lips. His giggles interrupt, so I run my hands through his hair and breathe deeply into the gap. He melts too. My body sinks heavy and slow, like lava down a slope, inching toward a deep crack. The room tilts forward, curving over the edge. I want to go with it, but he holds me back.

"It's your turn to choose a video."

I breathe in and turn around. The TV's a blur. The waves in the air make me sick. I sigh and fall sideways, landing on the couch with a pillow under my head as if I planned it that way. My flop of an arm fishes around for the remote as Steve squeezes in to spoon me from behind. I find the remote and fumble with the buttons.

"Do you want me to do it?"

"No!" The fire in my voice makes me laugh. Anger is funny when I'm drunk. Steve laughs too, but I kiss his hand because I know he doesn't quite understand. I choose a song from my youth and flip onto my back. My body cools as the steam escapes and the gray tune takes over. There is comfort in depression—I've always known this. My heart swells as the deep full-bodied voice sings and the amplified strings pull me back together. I feel like myself. I sing along, but Steve laughs, so I stop. I curl away as he shifts closer.

"Your turn." I hold the remote over my head. He takes it as I close my eyes. In the darkness, a violent beat explodes as an angry, whiny voice raps over. I smile and open my eyes. That red baseball hat never fails. The ingrained lyrics lift us both. I push off the cushion as Steve slides on his back to steady me on top. We sing together.

"I did it all for the nookie—come on! The nookie—come on!"

Our faces are charged with a ridiculous shared love. We make stupid faces as we rap along and throw our hands in the air. The synergy cuts through the fog. For a moment, my veins are clean and my eyes can see clear. I ease down close to him as we both start to kiss. Our lips together are soft and natural, but as gravity pushes me down, puffs of smoke suffocate the air. I pull away and open my eyes. The smoke is real. I lose all vision and hearing as the blackness takes me away.

I return to the room, still on top, still looking down, but there are tears in Steve's eyes. He turns away to the back of the couch as I try not to reveal what I've seen. We both need to hide from whatever occurred in the dark. I slide down and unbutton his pants, but his hand stops me.

"I better go."

"What? No. Stay."

His grip on the top of his jeans is firm. I crawl back up and slip my arms under his torso, knowing my strength. I lift him up, and his warmth returns. Within my arms, I can feel a rumble of glee.

"Where are you taking me?"

"Come on. Let's go."

His words resist, but they are meaningless fluff. I lead him easily by a hand into the bedroom to take off his shirt, his pants, and his socks. I toss my childhood bear aside to make room for him to slip under the sheet. With him secure, I flick off the light and strip fast, the way I do when I'm alone, and then I slide under the covers to cuddle naked beside his furry chest. He holds me like a cave. Neck craned back, I turn up to find his kiss. Neither of us need to hide on our sides. With my knees tucked, curled up small, and his body broad and all around, we fit perfectly.

"Can I ask you something?"

His words make me sleepy. I flip over to drift away.

"If we had met before last summer—before you met that guy—would things be different?"

The bed starts to spin. Under heavy lids, the nausea takes over. I clench the mattress and will the sickness down, but the memory foam is too soft. It flattens between my desperate fingers and sinks underneath me as I disappear deep down into a world of fabric silence and compressed sleep. I don't dream. I teleport instead to a different body, a different day, burning under the bright sun. I toss off the wet sheets to reveal my alien skin. I'm drenched. My head throbs as I rub at the pain and try to roll away, but a wall stops me. I back up to find Steve's eyes, open and penetrating as if they've been staring all night. My chest trembles. He giggles at the fear.

"Morning, drunkie."

Chapter Six

I tilt my chin down to the couch to conceal my smile.

"Would you like some tea?"

"Yes, please." Anything to distract her as I gain composure. My counselor moves into the hall as I peek into my purse, hooked by the glowing screen. Another text from Steve. A flurry of energy floats up from my spleen.

"So what's going on?"

I push my purse aside as she hands me the tea. The ceramic is hot, but still I tip the rim to my lips. My counselor sits down. I let the steam mask my face.

"You're beaming today!"

"Am I?" The liquid scalds my tongue. I place the mug aside and wipe the condensation from my face, flattening down my bubbled cheeks. The muscles resist. My smile reinflates. "Yeah, I guess I am."

"So what's up? Tell me everything!"

She holds her tea with both hands, seeping into the cupped warmth and the spilled delight flooding the room. I cross my legs and look to the slanted skylight. The sun shines in. I want to feel the rays. I want to believe in that outside light beaming through.

"I finally found something I want to do. You know, not just my usual *shoulds*."

"That's great news! What is it?"

I turn to her. My mouth opens, but I cover the gap and look away. I want to tell her everything, but Steve is consuming my mind. I bite my nail and tear off the sharp edge.

"I've started painting rocks."

Her chin holds out, but after a second of silence, she tucks back in to pull up a smile.

"Very cool! I love rocks! And painting is a wonderful outlet. Great way to relax too."

She's too sweet. I stare for a moment, wanting to tell her more, but my hands fidget in my lap. She notices.

"How has your anxiety been?"

I lock my hands together and look up. "Good. Well…definitely better."

She places her tea on the side table. "Has counting five objects helped?"

"Sort of." I chuckle and shake my head. "I feel crazy though when I do it. I'm glad no one can hear my thoughts."

"Aren't we all?" She smiles, her gaze too soft. I squeeze my crossed legs together and look to the hardwood floor. She leans in, crystal pendant swinging forward.

"So what else is going on? I could be wrong, but I'm sensing a bit of shame."

My body stiffens, bare legs cold as a new kind of flood pours in. I rub my hands over my knees as I force both feet down to the ground. I can't hide from the inevitable. Through a notch, an unwelcome smile coils in.

"Steve slept over last night."

"What? How did that happen? I thought you guys agreed to be just friends?" Her voice sends gentle waves of mirth down her shoulders and shawl. My smile confused her. "It's okay! You're allowed to like him."

"No, I can't. I can't like anybody."

"Why not?"

Pleading, I stare. She of all people should know. I shouldn't have to explain. My mind freezes as the past seals over. I try to extract the memory, but I can't go back. My body locks up.

"All feelings are innocent." Her sentiment turns cold in the air. I scratch my ear as the frost peppers down. I look away.

"Last night was stupid. It really didn't mean anything. I just got too drunk."

She taps her lip and lifts her chin. Her words come out slowly. "I hope you don't find this offensive, but would you consider yourself... *promiscuous?*"

The word stings. I pull back as the ice shatters and falls to the floor. The frozen layer coating my body was thinner than we both realized.

"I'm just curious! It's a common trait for people like y—with the same diagnosis."

"Steve and I didn't do anything. We only made out."

"Well, that sounds pretty PG to me." She smiles. I don't smile back. She turns to her tea, and I do the same, letting the hot water bite my tongue. I tilt the cup higher, liquid burning down my throat—a temperature to match the shame.

Senses muddled, I put the drink down. "I'm actually thinking about becoming abstinent."

She lifts her head. "Interesting. What made you decide that?"

The lamp flashes bright for a moment—a bulb of painful white bursting in. The light dims as the sterile smell disappears and the earth-toned room returns. The hard swivel chair fluffs back to the seat beneath my counselor.

"I just want to be alone." I look down to shadow my face. "I don't want to need anyone...or hurt anybody."

She crosses her legs and leans back in her chair. I watch carefully as she breathes in. She nods and sighs. "I have something I'd like you to try when you get home. Have you ever heard of the 'what's the consequence of that' exercise?"

I shake my head.

"Okay. So this is your homework assignment. After dinner or whenever you feel comfortable, I want you to ask yourself what it would mean if you liked Steve. Don't answer now. I want you to write everything down later. Be as honest as you can and then ask yourself, 'What's the consequence of that?' Repeat this process and keep going for as long as you need to."

"Okay..." I don't really understand.

"The whole point of the exercise is to reach a place of calm. Eventually, you'll run out of answers, and the idea that set off the series of questions won't seem so stressful anymore."

My hands squeeze together in my lap. I wish I never brought up Steve. I should have kept these thoughts to myself.

"But you can explore that later. Right now, I wanna hear more about you. I love that you've found a hobby you enjoy! Have you shared your painted rocks with your friends?"

"No." I hesitate. "I'm kinda keeping that to myself... Don't worry though! I am seeing my friends. We have plans to hang out this weekend."

"Fun! Are these the friends you made online?"

A laugh puffs out. "Yeah." It all sounds so sad.

"No, that's great! What are you girls gonna do?"

"Probably go out in Providence. It's what we always do."

She cocks her head. "Is that what *you* wanna do?"

"No," I laugh. The cracked-open truth splatters on the floor. "But I know I have to see them. I can't stay in every night with my cat."

I smile at the thought and the humorous mess on the ground, but my counselor gazes past it all, sadness in her eyes. The spreading yolk on the floor reverses, sucking back up into the shell as the cracks close. I swallow the egg of truth back down. The lump drops heavy into my chest.

"What about your other friends?"

My eyes drip down. "Yeah, Erin's cool, but Laura moved away. She lives in Massachusetts now with a boyfriend, so I don't really see her."

"That's too bad. You and her seemed to have a lot in common."

"Yeah..." The wood softens beneath my feet as I sink down. Black mold rots the floor as an erosion takes place inside. None of my friends fill the void. None of my friends even compare. I breathe in sharply, remembering Steve.

"It's okay, though. I'll have fun Saturday and then spend the rest of the weekend alone."

She smiles. "That sounds like a good plan."

We both prefer to end on a positive note. She gets up and moves to her desk to flip open her planner. Once a month is all I can afford, but she never seems to mind. I hand her the money as we agree on our next date.

"Let me know how that exercise goes tonight. I think it'll be interesting."

I hug her goodbye and then exit down the stairs. Across the street, I stop at the natural remedies store to buy a couple candles—a homework assignment I skipped before—and then I head home to run a bath. With the wicks lit and the tub filling, I sit on the couch with a notebook and pen. My cat squeezes in between as I start to write.

What would it mean if I liked Steve?

I drift to the side to think. The torrent gushes loud behind me. The water from the bathroom fills my ears.

It would mean I'm weak—that I'm not strong enough to be on my own.

My eyes focus in on the smudged word. A text dings, and my heart chimes. I ball my hands into fists as the water churns. I never keep my phone on sound.

And what's the consequence of being weak?

No thought required. My pen answers for me.

I wouldn't feel proud. I would never become the independent person I've always wanted to be.

And what's the consequence of that?

I would be a failure.

And the consequence of that?

I would be ashamed. I would hate myself. I would become depressed again.

My pen is vicious. It scribbles across the page.

Consequence of that?

Never accomplish my dreams.

Consequence of that?

Unhappy. Unfulfilled. Never forgive myself.

Consequence of that?

The ink bleeds my fingertips dry. I turn to the bath—to the muted current. The water has reached the top. I get up quickly to stop the flow, and then I return to read the bottom of the page.

Die regretful and sad.

"Jesus!" I laugh. Not exactly the answer my counselor was hoping for. I close the notebook to try out the bath instead. My hand dips first into the water, disappointed by the lukewarm temperature. I strip down anyway and step inside, breathing in too much, too frequently in an attempt to appreciate the candles' scent. I stare into the wiggly flame. Its light is small, but it's enough to illuminate the blacked-out memory from last night.

"None of this is fake. My feelings for you are real."

I dunk under the water and splash out quickly to escape drowning. I pull out the plug and force the tub to drain, using my wet fingers to snuff out all the candles and my remembered words.

Chapter Seven

I start the ignition and the radio explodes, volume full blast. I crank the dial down and breathe in. My hands are shaking, temples heavy. From the open window upstairs, my cat cries, calling me back inside. She doesn't realize how much I want to stay. All I want to do is lie in bed and block out last night, but I can't. I have to forge ahead and get out of this routine.

My stomach gurgles as I back out of the driveway and head onto the road, but the sounds are deceiving. I want food. My mouth and brain both beg, but my gut is a bloated reminder that food is the last thing I need. I roll down the window to air out the stale stench of salted grease. The steering wheel slides with a sheen under my hands. I pull down the sleeve of my hoodie to wipe away the oil, but I can still feel the crystallized crumbs under my nails. Despite my pounding headache, I turn up the music and suck in the breeze, hoping the drive and distance will be enough to make me feel better.

"I need heavier rocks."

A pothole bumps my backpack off the seat and rattles my painted stones. I pull the empty bag back up and run my fingers over the smooth, detailed paintings. I should feel high. I felt high yesterday when I checked the weather and decided on this extra step, but that was before I saw my friends. I rub my neck and squeeze at the lumps in my throat, straining to keep my eyes on the road ahead. Over the bridge to Little Compton, the wind changes, slowing down as it makes its way through tall grassy fields. I ease off the gas and look around. To my left, farm-stands pass—worn wooden signs painted above fresh offerings and humble tin cans. There are no people. The hills of grass spread across on either side, breathing open space between the houses and room in my ears. I turn the music down and lean over to roll open my passenger window. The warmed earth and hints of cool waves cleanse the air, lifting my mind to a different kind of craving. I smile and sing, remembering my purpose, returning to that higher place.

The road curves left along a beach and comes to a crowded parking lot. I pull in and take the last space along the wall bordering the sand. I park but keep the engine running as I stare out at the colorful array of blankets and bikinied bodies. *Why did I think I'd be alone?* Under my hoodie, my armpits sweat, but I can't take it off. My tank top is skintight. I bunch up the sleeves and take out my phone to search for a quieter beach. I tap the GPS and drift aimlessly around the map—elementary colors, pale blue and splotches of green. I know what they mean, but I don't know what I'm looking for. My thumb floats away and taps instead on the photo app. Snapshots from last night. Through my open window, baked sunscreen and small plastic wheels on pavement roll by too close. I seal out the intrusion, closing the window to turn on the AC as I zoom in on the still life in my palm. My smile looks real. In every picture, all my teeth are showing, wide on a carefree face, dressed and made up to blend in. I look the way I imagined myself to be at this age when I was thirteen: decorated in jewelry, steady in heels, and surrounded by friends in a lively bar. I zoom out and hold the phone away, trying to see myself through younger eyes, but the pressure over my waistband distracts. I suck in and pull up my leggings. I wish my mind captured memories like my phone.

I blacken the screen and toss it aside, cutting off the unphotographed end. My saliva remembers. I swallow the thick sweetness—the butter-coated vomit—and grab my floppy backpack before shutting off the car. I step onto the beach as my body jiggles and my sneakers kick up sand. Everyone is watching. With my head down, I can feel their eyes. Still, I keep my pace controlled through the crowd, remembering the kids in school—the ones who used to run home from the bus, book bags flapping up and down like a foolish cape. They didn't hear the laughter, but I did.

On the far end of the beach, free from the people, my breath returns. The sand stretches all the way to Westport—a mile of solitude expanding open my chest. The wind over the crest of the waves doesn't judge the rolls it sweeps over. With each step, I feel lighter and closer to myself.

The dunes peak and lower to reveal an untamed marsh on my left. My path gravitates to the tall grass, drawn to the safety between the reeds, but also toward the hill of distant trees. I stop and stare. The backdrop doesn't seem real. As I scale the mountain in my mind and try to imagine walking within those wild leaves, a cavity deepens at the bottom of my chest. I inhale, but the hole opens wider. I want to consume the entire scene and at the same time disappear and become a part of it. The longing for the backdrop is overwhelming. I look down. Bleached and scattered along the soft sand lay several rocks. I pick one up and smile. The rock is warm and heavy cradled in my hand, ten times the size of my painted stones—exactly what I was looking for. I take the largest ones and zipper them inside my backpack. A few feet ahead, I find several more. I don't stop until I collect all sixteen.

I drop the rocks inside the open bag and zipper them up. I take the straps and lift without bending my knees.

"Jesus!"

The monstrosity falls. The rocks clop together as they hit the sand. I leave them there as I survey the distance ahead—the steps and stares back to the parking lot. I can't avoid the crowd. There's no way they won't notice me this time. I look down at the backpack again, remembering my counselor's words.

There's no way around your problems. The only way to get over them is to go through.

Breathing in, I squat down and lift the backpack, this time ready for the weight. I heave the load onto my back and click the front buckles around. The rocks settle at the bottom as I hunch over. I lift my elbows over my head to hold the top, pulling the weight up by my arms like a crane. I move forward. Head down, eyes on my feet, I can hear the crowd coming. I smile as an old belief returns: nobody else is real. I pass through the detached voices along my own separate channel, moving easily like the one true avatar in a video game. They can't touch me. They can't hurt me. The idea carries me back to the car.

I dump the bag of rocks behind my front seat and get in. The heat trapped inside is unbreathable. I turn the key and blast the AC, tearing my hoodie off over my head. The air cools my bare arms.

"Ahhh."

I lean my shoulders into the relief, rocking side to side as the temperature turns colder. The tingles spread across. Hot to cold, my skin is awakened by the extremes.

I turn up my music and sing loud as I drive back home. I float over the field this time, flying higher than the blades of grass can reach. Everything is energizing. With my rocks in the back and my plan's momentum back up to pace, the road moves on its own. It takes me to a small café I've never been. I leave my backpack and hoodie in the car, taking only my wallet and phone.

On the patio overlooking a river, I sit outside with my coffee. I drag another chair closer to stretch out my legs as I steady myself to take in the view. With no one else around, the water sparkles. I drink too fast, sucking the ice at the bottom of my coffee and ending on an airy sip. I pop open the lid to crunch the ice. As I chew, the river comes in jumpy frames. I lift my phone to capture the beauty, but my sister's name pops across the screen.

I look down and read her text. A stream of several more pour in—they're all long. My thumb scrolls carefully as I read down the blocks of words. Invisible waves wiggle the screen. *Creg*. Heat simmers at the back of my ribs, down in a secret place. I sigh and look away. I knew he would change. I knew it the day she took me aside. The current in the river flattens, and the glimmer disappears as I remember the words.

"I think he's the one."

I shake the ice and let the shards fill my mouth. The plastic cup collapses in my fist. I throw it away and return to my car, swapping out the CD for an album of a lower vibration.

Chapter Eight

My sister's car is already here. I park as close as I can and check my phone.

> Hey, Miss! Got here early. I'm at the bar on the third floor.

The sliver of mint crunches between my teeth as I examine my makeup in the mirror. A lot can change in an hour's drive. I separate a stubborn lash, clung by mascara to another, and apply a fresh coat of lip gloss before stepping out. The parking attendant waves as I walk by, but I don't mind the attention. I pop a fresh mint in my mouth as I ascend the stairs, holding up my long black dress to make way for my strappy heels.

On the top floor, I spot my sister: bun frizzy and flopped on top, shoulders covered up and hunched forward. The energy from my cheeks drains. I pull up the front of my scoop neckline, controlling my hips as I move closer. She turns—a spark ignites in her eyes but immediately dulls.

"Wow, Miss, you look amazing."

I brush off a stray dog hair and slip quickly in the seat beside. Her fingers fiddle in her lap, cracked polish curtained by delicate fabrics and layers of mismatched colors. I hang my purse on the back of the chair, steadying myself into her puffed, unmade eyes.

"You do too."

"Jeez! If I had known you were gonna get all dressed up, I wouldn't have come straight from the beach."

I shake my head and grab the edge of the bar, pulling closer to tuck myself underneath.

"No, Man, you're beautiful." My words are soft. I watch them float down like petals over her face. They shouldn't have to fall. I swallow the remnants of peppermint and curve forward, arms crossed on the bar. Her glass is empty. I grab the menu to look over the drinks. "So how are you?"

She sighs. "I don't know. It's been such a stressful week. Thanks for meeting me last minute by the way."

"Of course." I put the menu down. "I had an easy dog walking day, so it was no problem."

"Thank god I have you, Miss. I don't know what I would do without you."

She smiles, a lifetime of pain in her eyes. The bartender relieves me from the depth.

"Can I get you something to drink?"

My sister pushes her glass toward him. "I'll take another margarita."

He nods and then looks back at me. "And for you?"

"Yeah, I'll do the same."

"Sounds good." His smile lingers as he holds my eyes. I break the gaze and turn toward my sister. My jaw loosens as he walks away.

"Okay, so do you want to talk about what happened or would you rather…?"

She breathes in through her nose. "No, I definitely need to talk about it. The whole situation has been driving me insane."

My fingers fiddle, pulling up and down my rings. "Why? What's going on?"

She slurps up the watery remnants of her drink and then touches her face. "I'm so confused. I don't understand Creg. We were supposed to hang out tonight, but he canceled last minute, just like he did last time."

"What was his excuse? Reason! Sorry."

The drinks come. We both reach out and take a sip.

"No, it's okay, Miss. I kind of think it was an excuse too." She picks up her phone. "Let me just read you what he said…"

I poke at the ice with my straw and twirl the drink as she searches. Her voice flattens as she reads. Her body stays close to the phone.

Hey. Sorry, I just got out of work and I think tonight I'm gonna stay in and go to bed early. Gotta work at 4:00 a.m. tomorrow.

I wait, but the gap turns to silence. She looks at me.

"Okay, well that's pretty understandable, if it's true. He does work odd hours."

"Yeah, but that's what he said last time, and then at one or two in the morning, he started posting stuff to Facebook, so *clearly* he was still up." Her mouth shuts, and her eyes freeze, suddenly wide. She retreats to her lap, squeezing her hands together. "I know that sounds creepy. I hate that I even know that. I don't know what's wrong with me."

"Nothing's wrong with you." I place my hand on her back, but the touch doesn't feel right. I look down as my arms shrivel back to my side. "If anyone understands, it's me."

My pebbled words are like embers to her fire.

"Exactly! I actually thought of you the other day when his ex started blowing me up with all that stuff about how he's only using me to get back at her. Creg says she's crazy, but I feel sorry for her."

My eyelids squeeze. A cold stiffness takes over. I grab my drink and pinch a clump of salt from the rim, letting the crystals shock the tip of my tongue. "Yeah, I don't know. That's a weird situation."

"It's *so* weird. Yeah this is what she said…"

I drink steadily, eyes on the bar, as she rereads the texts she already sent me. At the bottom of my glass, I swirl down. I want to melt and slip away, but her voice clenches me to the seat. The bartender glances up from the far side. Everyone's listening. People are staring. My sister doesn't notice—all senses glued to her phone.

"Would you ladies like to order some food?"

She snaps up from the screen and then looks at me. "What are you getting?"

I place my hand on my flat stomach, feeling the empty warmth. The tequila soothes back. "Honestly, I'm fine skipping dinner. I'll take another drink, though."

"What? No. You have to eat." Her eyes plead, invisible arms reaching out as my chair sails away. The distance hurts. Against the current, I let her pull me back, ordering the same meal as her.

"Two fajita salads and another round of drinks coming right up." The bartender winks at me before walking away. I shake off the subtlety and return to my sister.

"Well, I'm happy you're here. Anything's better than sitting at home, ruminating about all this. It's important to get out and have your own life. That's what I've learned..."

"You're right, Miss." She puts the phone down. "I really do need my own life again. I used to be so independent. Now all I do is think about him. I'm always waiting! Waiting for him to call, waiting for him to get out of work, wondering what he's really up to."

My mouth twitches. I scan the room for my next drink. She finishes off hers and sighs. "Thank *god* for school. Homework and classes keep me sane."

Jaw tight, I breathe in. "Yeah. How's that going?"

"Good! A lot of work though. Grad school is intense. You should see my DSM book. It's *filled* with underlines and Post-its."

"Mm, yeah, I bet." I search the room again. The bartender pops out from the back with our food and drinks on a tray. I push the napkin and empty glass aside to make room.

"Here you are, ladies. Can I get you two anything else?"

"No, I think we're good." I flash a smile, but he walks away. My face solidifies back to stone. I pick up my fork and stab a piece of chicken as my sister continues.

"And I still love my internship, but I'm definitely ready to move on from kids and work with adults. All the good stuff you say about your counselor really inspires me."

I sit up and swallow fast. "Really? That's awesome! She's the best. I don't know what I would do without her."

"That's so cool. I wanna be like her."

A puff of warm fuzz expands throughout my body as I gaze at my sister. Her flowy sleeves remind me of my counselor—motherly arms shawled in delicate femininity, collected and worn over miles of experience and travel. A gypsy. I trust those kind of hearts.

"Can I share something with you?"

"Of course! Anything, Miss."

Within this moment of tipsy love, her words sound genuine. I lean in. "I came up with an idea the other day. A way to understand and deal with my problems."

"Oh? Okay. What do you mean?" She turns to her salad to eat as I talk—a skill I still don't understand. "Go on."

"I…uh…I got these rocks that I'm gonna carry around. They're supposed to represent my burdens." Eyes on the bowl, she shovels and chews. I poke feebly at the lettuce. "I was actually supposed to start carrying them today…"

Suddenly, a song sweeps the room. The volume is loud, both in my mind and my sister's ear. She puts her utensils down and smiles.

"Oh my god—Miss, I'm so sorry to interrupt, but I can't help it. You know how much I love this song!"

Her hands sway and swim in the air, just like they did at the music festival. The fluid moves through me. I don't mind the change.

"It's okay. I totally understand."

I sip my drink to sway too. We both dance in our seat, arms in the air, free and connected along a shared tempo. I hum as she sings.

"Miss, I've missed you."

"I've missed you too. We need to do this more often."

The song ends, and she floats back down to eat, but I have no interest in food. I graze the top layer of my salad as she works her way to the ceramic bottom. All I want to do now is drink.

"Do you want to go to another bar after this?"

A song from the speakers curls up my spine, but she doesn't feel it. I stop dancing.

"I wish, Miss, but I'm exhausted. I really need to go home."

"Yeah, you're right. I should too."

The check comes, laid between us heavy in a black pleather case. We slide our plastic cards in and wait for the final step.

"So are you going straight home after this or do you have pet sitting to do…?"

"No. I'm going straight home."

"Good, I'm glad."

She smiles, lips tight. I breathe in deep and twist my lips, angry at the fear inside. I push it down and try to act pleasant, but the booze is starting to turn.

"Thank you, ladies. Have a wonderful night."

The bartender's words are aimed now at my sister. My smile fails. He won't look at me. I sign the check and then ease off the stool, following the lead of my long nonsensical dress. My clunky heels catch the bottom. I hike up the hindrance and walk carefully toward the stairs, holding the railing the whole way down.

Back in the parking lot, my balance returns. The night air cools down the tension and opens my arms wide. I hug my sister.

"I love you, Man, so, so much."

"I love you too! Thanks again for meeting up with me."

"Anytime." I pull away and look her in the eye. She's five inches taller than me, but right now, we feel the same. "You're too good for him. You deserve the best because you are the best."

"Aw, thanks for saying that, Miss. Yeah, I'll let you know how that goes."

She hugs fast once more and then returns to her car. I watch her get in before walking back to mine. She doesn't back out until I turn my headlights on. I follow her to the exit, and then we go our separate ways. The back roads lead to the highway, the highway leads to swerving thoughts and tempting signs. For forty minutes, I grit my teeth, but off the exit, the reduced speed takes away my willpower. I pull off the road and crawl underneath the illuminated arch—my own secret heaven. The light hits my cup holder as I cross under. I toss the bottle into the back before pulling up to the window to grab my greased paper bag. I eat as I drive. I eat as I listen. I eat to deafen the sound of the empty beer bottle, rolling back and forth between the discarded trash.

Chapter Nine

My eyes flash open, and I breathe in. My cat is staring. She's wide awake, sitting in front of me. The sheets are soaked. Heart racing, I roll away from the cold sweat stains and wipe the streaks from my forehead. The room seems disturbingly aware—too silent and listening. I think I was talking in my sleep.

I strip the bed and dump the sheets in the back room. I can't deal with laundry right now. I have a busy day—so much to get through before I can get back to my projects.

I eat breakfast and pack up the car with everything I need: my backpack, my rocks, a brand-new journal, and one of my painted stones. As I drive to my first pet sitting stop, the sour spots and tension from my dream start to fade. I pile the leather journal, a pen, the stone, and a key in my hands and ascend the three flights of stairs to join the cat at the very top. The sun has only just risen above the trees.

The slender tortoiseshell greets me with her usual long, single-toned series of meows. I put my stuff down on the coffee table to pick her up. I hold her close. Her chatty mouth continues to sing.

"You are so stinking cute!" I kiss her on the cheek. She pulls back to look at me, and I laugh. She hasn't seen me since my waterfall of ideas. All my animals have reacted the same. They can't figure out why my eyes are so green.

I kiss her once more before placing her back on the ground. She follows me to the litter box, the water bowl and feeding dish, and then jumps up to join me on the couch. I only need to stay for thirty minutes, but I've carved out an hour for the sake of my project. I grab my journal from the table and run my hand over the leather binding. Embossed on the front, there is a dragon, much like the dragons I used to draw when I was a kid. I look around. The room makes me giddy. On the side table, next to the navy blue couch, a pink block of salt holds a tea candle. Hanging above and all around me, ivy plants grow wild, flowing over suspended pots and twisting around exposed beams. The light isn't bright in here—there's only one window, and it faces south—but it's enough. I pick up the painted stone and study it in my hand. Then I reach for the pen.

The cat rubs her cheek against the journal, letting the stiff corner bump over her teeth. She bites. I bite too. I chew the hollow cap of my pen, knowing what I want to write but feeling torn as I do. The dream from this morning keeps distracting me. I take the stone from the table again and flip it to the back: "Fleeting Innocence." I wrote this with a clear event in mind, but the purple butterfly on the front means so much more. I spread my fingertips across my forehead, nails pushing paths in the skin, and turn to the window. The sky is lighter. The clouds are losing their mysterious morning glow. I sigh. I don't want to leave this place. I wish I could cut out everything mundane and work solely on this project.

I force the tip of the pen back to the page, but my phone lights up with a text. It's Erin. I hold my breath as I read her message:

> Want to join me and Kate for the outdoor movie tonight? They're playing the Mr. Rogers documentary!

I twist and nibble at the inside of my cheek. I know I should go. I need to say yes. I reply and flip the phone down as the nerves start to stir. The cat watches silently as the high I felt when I first walked in sucks out my chest into the flipped-over block on the table. The phone, the brightening window—they both feel like vacuums.

Time slips by fast as I return to my journal. By the end of the hour, my pen is in full control. I haven't written anything about the rock. The ink flowed steadily, but as I flip back over the five pages, the only thing I find is the messy dream. I can't read it. I close the journal and gather the rest of my belongings to head back downstairs.

As I walk the dogs, I follow my planner as usual, but my mind is somewhere else. The sidewalks feel too straight. My pen can't cross out the scheduled part of my day fast enough. When I finally reach the blank space, I breathe. I open my windows and flip back the sunroof part of my soft top to let in the warm breeze. I drive out of town, down East Main Road, allowing the pavement to guide as the wind lifts me to a higher place. I turn right down a street I've never seen and a little ways down, a wooden sign marks the entrance to a trail. I pull into the empty lot, smiling at this secret pocket in the woods.

"This is perfect. Exactly what I need."

I step out and slide the front seat forward. In the back, my rocks are all ready. I grab the handle of the backpack and lug out the weight. The rocks shift and hang low inside. My muscles shake as I haul the bag onto my back.

"Definitely a burden!"

The leaves flutter, laughing with me. I click the front straps around and hunch forward to hike up the rocks. I grab my phone and secure the earbuds in, pressing play on the song my sister and I danced to at the bar before heading out into the trees.

The growth is dense along the path, but even underneath the shade of the mature leaves, I start to sweat. I wipe away the beads and grip the shoulder straps. My back is bent, head down, legs swollen with the sudden need for strength. I push forward, eyes on the dirt, trying to focus on the music, but the beat is too light. It doesn't match my pounding feet. I continue on as the sun blazes open the trail, bursting away the trees to a sunburnt field. Through squinted eyes, I look around. The sweat beads fast. I can't keep up with the trickles. They tickle down lightly like the rhythmic worm inside my ears. I pull out my phone from the waist pocket and search for a different song. A playlist from eighth grade scrolls by. I open it up and hit shuffle, nodding to the heavy beat. My feet march forward as a devilish smile creeps in. The rageful lyrics match the impact on my knees.

"Supercharged."

As I hike, the smile persists, and without a soul nearby, there's no need to hide. My biceps bulge, locked against the weight, squeezing in the straps. I charge through another patch of woods with my gaze forward and steady. The trail weaves through a meadow and along a vacant soccer field before looping back around. An hour has passed by the time I reach the parking lot, but I almost feel like turning around. The old awakened energy still rages inside. I pull out my earbuds and feel the heightened strength start to drain.

The ground rumbles from behind. I quickly take off my backpack as a car pulls in and parks beside me. I jump in and lock my door, smiling fast as the man spots me and waves. I wait. A lab barks and follows him onto the trail. Once they're gone, I pull down the mirror to analyze my face. The faded scar near my chin, the dark patches on my upper lip—they're both still there. I check the clock. An hour to go before I promised to meet Erin. I drive home fast to shower and cover up, applying the concealer heavily. I get back in my car and drive to the lot next to the crowded field for the outdoor movie. A hundred people stare as I approach, but Erin waves from a blanket in the back. A flood of relief pours in. I hurry up the hill, flexing my bicep secretly under the sleeve, trying to remember the strength from before.

"Well, hello." Erin pats the space beside her, so I sit down. Kate leans over from the other end. "You two have met, right?"

"Yeah." Kate smiles. "I think once before."

We've met twice, but I don't say anything. There's no need to look back. I'd rather we all forget last summer.

"So how's it going, little lady? You look like you've been getting a lot of sun."

"Do I?" My cheeks flush. I can feel the sweat speckling my upper lip, but I can't smear the makeup. I hate how nervous people make me feel. "Probably from dog walking. Busy day. How are you guys?"

"Good! Yeah, Kate and I were just talking about how excited we are for summer. Can't wait to go out and see people again."

"We've both been cocooning."

The tremble in my smile steadies. I didn't expect such honesty from so soft a voice. Kate's delicate blond hair lifts discretely at the ends. Erin's short ponytail whips around.

"Yep. Time to get out and start dating! Speaking of, how's Mr. Steve?"

My face crumbles in the spotlight. I gather my smile back quickly. "He's good. We're still just friends, though."

"Mmm, and how's *that* going?"

The curve in the corner of her lips is subtle, but released in the air, the movement snakes. I can't lie. I know she and Steve talk without me. I look down to the blanket. "Yeah, I messed up the other night, but that won't happen again."

"Wait, sorry, who's Steve again?"

Kate looks back and forth. I look to Erin. I feel like she should explain.

"Steve's the guy I met when I first moved here. He's the sweetest! Melissa and him would make the cutest pair." She turns to me. "But I totally understand where you're coming from. It's too soon. But he sure does like *you*."

Her last word drags on too long. She catches the wince and turns to Kate. As a bubble forms around them both, I roll up my sleeves and look around. The sky is darkening. The evening air cools my skin. I watch the inflated screen sway smoky gray at the bottom of the hill, sending out a stream of eerie waves. No one else seems to notice. The disturbance ripples invisible through the crowd, creeping closer but never quite touching my skin. I pull my feet in from the grass and look up. A ghost walks toward me. My cheeks sink as my breath stops and the world hollows. There's nowhere else to look. I'm trapped in a tunnel, staring as the figure turns around and sits down. She's real. The tunnel opens. She's real, and she's sitting exactly how I dreamed, right in front of me.

Erin turns to me. I don't have time to hide.

"Hey, are you okay?"

I swallow and regain my breath. My voice comes out low and flat. "Erin, this is gonna sound crazy, but my dream from last night just came true."

"What? What do you mean?"

I peek up to make sure the ghost isn't listening. I can't tell. Her hair is thick and longer than mine. "I had a dream about Allie. I dreamt all this. The hill, the blankets, the people around us. The setting was the same, and just like in the dream, she's sitting right there."

Erin follows my gaze. Her eyes grow wide.

"Wait, that's Allie? The one with dark hair?"

I nod.

"Hey, what's going on?"

A cool shock hits my ears. Kate's too loud. I want to expand the bubble and let her in, but it's not safe.

Erin cocks her head. "Do you mind if I tell her?"

I nod under her heightened stance, unsure of what I just agreed to. Her body turns away, weaving Kate into a nest of whispers. I try not to watch. I try not to hear as my own string of words thread from Erin's mouth and pull out my chest from the original spool. The virus spreads. Kate gasps and leans forward to look at me.

"Oh my gosh! That's terrible! I'm so sorry. What an awful friend."

"Yeah." My response is small, but it drags like a dagger coming out. Erin touches my back. Her open palm on my sweatshirt thinks it understands, but underneath the cotton, everything is more complicated.

"Here." Kate hands me some vodka and a cup of soda.

"Ooh yes!" Erin pats my back. "Drink up. You'll feel better."

I unscrew the cap and let the thick clarity glug in. I tip the edge of the cup to disappear inside. My lashes glow blue. The screen at the bottom of the hill is alive, ready to begin. I let the amplified sound numb over as the movie draws all attention away. The crowd becomes the background. As the night sky slips over, the hill fades to black and all the people become bodiless heads, a sea of lumps outlined beneath the screen. I want to become a silhouette too. I force myself out toward the movie, but the giants on the screen seem to be talking to me. Mr. Rogers speaks, "Love is at the root of everything—all learning, all parenting, all relationships. Love or the *lack* of it."

The word flashes red. Down in the dark, my eyes take a moment to adjust, but soon I find Allie again, sitting so close, so real and so still. I want to get up. I want to reach out and talk to her, but I know I can't because of the dream. In the end, she screamed. I tried to explain—begged her to forgive—but she wouldn't listen. She acted just like me.

I swallow up the last of my drink to drown out the rage. *I'm better off without her.* That's what my journal said. That's what I have to believe.

Chapter Ten

The traffic on Farewell Street finally breaks as I speed up the ramp and head over the bridge. The drive to escape has been building all week. I breathe in, drawn up by the rising suspension chords, rolling open my window to blow away the town behind me and all the people who don't understand. Their laden eyes and loaded questions weigh heavy on my side. Beyond the Jamestown Bridge, the fear finally leaves as my foot lightens off the gas pedal.

I sigh and look around. The sky is clear. Alive in the sun, the trees guide me light green and shaded two-toned leaves along the highway. The world has dimension again. I drift off the exit, away from Narragansett, away from route one, away from all the people as I follow the green. I don't know where I'm going. All I know is I need to find a new place—somewhere undiscovered to unload my first rock.

At the red light, the stillness seeps in. I plug in my phone and hit shuffle, skipping the first few songs. The light changes. I turn left and the music starts to play. Small popping bubbles rise up my face to the upbeat melody, but the feeling fizzles out. Face flat again, I skip the song. The next ten do the same.

"Where the fuck is my music?"

I search as I follow the back roads, tapping away tainted albums and driving past familiar trees. The sun grows rounder, slipping occasionally behind the taller trees. I should have left earlier. The clock on my radio reflects an anxious green. I tap the skip button rapidly—too fast for my phone to keep up—and then I toss it aside to settle on whatever it finds. Heavy drums, solid bass, and my favorite raspy voice. I nod and smile. This song is mine. I sing and scream along, reunited with my old friends, but through the fire, an intruder steps in. I sing louder, trying to scare the memory away, but his laugh takes over. Steve had never been in a mosh pit before, but he wasn't afraid. He loved it just as much as me.

I punch the volume knob off and hold my fist in the air with a sigh puffed and loaded in my cheeks. The fumes escape. My arm goes down. I try to focus on the road—the straight yellow line and the curbed sides—but my thoughts aren't as easily contained. I drive for an hour and see nothing, all my senses focused in on my hands. I grip the steering wheel, resisting the urge to reach for my phone, but my fingers soften as my mind melts across the pavement and drips over the side to dead leaves. *Steve loves the woods. He and I have that in common.* On the side of the road, a large wooden sign snaps me back—a swift slap across the face.

Arcadia Management Area.

The white letters are bold. I pull into the dirt lot as the pines unfold and tower around. Their essence seeps in: sweet, spiced air. I park and breathe in deep, smiling at the empty space and my good fortune. I step out and stand for a moment, giddy underneath the golden rays and absorbed soft brown warmth beneath my shoes. I look to the main path—it curves dusty and wide into the trees, similar to a trail my mom used to take me to as a child. I remember her voice back then—it was soothing. I breathe and walk to the other side of my car to load my rocks onto my back, zippering my phone quickly inside the waist strap pocket. I kiss the butterfly painted stone and place it back on the seat, shutting the door to lock it behind.

"I'll keep the painted stones as reminders."

The rocks shift and weigh heavy on my hips as I walk away. I tighten the shoulder straps and cinch the band closer across my chest, but the weight still feels heavy on my sides. Stopped at the trailhead, I wiggle up the bottom of the bag as I stare at the map, pretending to read. I don't want to know. When I was a kid, I never stopped to care. I forge ahead, summoning my youth as I brave into the trees, away from the sunbaked tire tracks into the shadowed unknown. I gaze up the spiked pines, watching the bark grow veins and the needles sharpen with each cumbersome step. I look down. I'm not supposed to be afraid. My body has grown, but somehow inside, I've turned into a coward.

I stick to the main path, bypassing the smaller trails that weave like snakes through the weeds. Up ahead, I can see exactly where I'm going. I count my steps as I trek forward, watching the wide dirt road like a never-ending treadmill beneath my feet. Bored, I reach for my phone. No messages. Steve is quiet today. I hover, considering a million things I want to tell him, but instead, I zipper away the urge and force the bad habit aside.

After two thousand muttered steps, a moth flutters by my face. I swat the nuisance away and snort out a breath, but it comes back, a little further away this time. The purple wings pump in the air.

"Whoa, you're really beautiful."

I reach out to touch, but like confetti, it floats down. As I stand, another set of soft wings join, followed by two more.

"Purple butterflies. Just like my stone."

The words come out without me asking. I only realize the significance as the sound hits the air. I grab my phone. I need proof. I need to capture this, but as I fumble to pull up the camera, the butterflies drift away.

"Crap!"

I follow them into the weeds, pushing aside thorns and dangling vines. I snap through a branch. All around me, slithered with a three-pronged tongue, poison ivy coats the trees. I back out carefully, avoiding their glistening touch. I am a fool to have followed. I am a fool to have believed. Back on the main path, I regain my pace and my predictable breath. I march on, head down, back strained, cursing my naivety in the kicked-up puffs of stinging sand. Tears burn, but I don't let them fall. Hands around the straps, I squeeze the weight in and keep it clenched until I reach a fork in the path.

Shaded and narrow, the trail on the left leads down a slope. My gaze drips toward the dark, but I snap it back to the sunny dirt hill to the right. I force myself to hike toward the light, but the pebbles roll down behind my boots as my instincts pull away.

"Screw this." I turn around and walk steadily down the shadowed path. The crooked branches scrape the top of my bag and gather me in. They pat like an old friend's arm, ushering me back.

Through the leaves, I can barely see, but somewhere close, a brook follows my path. The bubbling current carries me on. I listen to it as I walk fast, snapping twigs and elbowing aside distracting things. The trees step back. The path curves left suddenly and opens wide. I move close to the dark and silent edge. The water here is still. I lean over the black liquid glass to pour my reflection in. I am a shade—an unrecognizable self.

I sigh. "This is the place."

I unbuckle my backpack and prop it up against a tree. Across the water, the shore on the other side is near. I unzip the bag and dig out my heaviest rock. The weight is smooth. I pull my arm back to throw, but the rock slips down and thumps to the dirt. I pick it up. Beach dust powders my hands.

"You don't belong here. This isn't your home."

I cup the rock in both hands and breathe in the remnants of salted sea. I close my eyes and open again. Down the brook a bit further, the current picks up.

I leave my backpack behind and creep along the mucky edge toward the row of moss-covered stones. I step to the first one easily, but the second is too far to reach. I look to the brook between and my semi-waterproof boots.

"Eh, fuck it."

I step in, letting the water drench my shoes. The seeping cold makes me laugh. My laces weren't prepared. My wool socks try to repel, but my feet wiggle the feeling in. I climb up the slippery side of the innermost rock and prop myself on top to sit and breathe.

The front of my skull softens and expands. With each breath, the moss under my seat cradles me deeper. My body's boundaries start to fuzz as the rock in my hand separates. I look to the solid anomaly. I turn it over in my hands.

"Innocence must die for something greater to be born."

The words whisper through me. I watch their subtle current twirl off my lips like fiddleheads connected in the air. The rock absorbs the gentle wind. The weight is the same, but the meaning is brand new.

I sigh and place it down, letting its underside darken in the wet moss, and then I make my way back to shore. I pick up my bag and secure the buckles, but my eyes turn back to gaze once more. The bleached rock stands like an idol—a treasure traveled far from a distant land. I smile and move on, floating back to my car in half the time. I take my backpack off and lay it down on the floor behind my seat. I get in. I watch the sky turn dark gray. The rain starts to pour.

"This is amazing! It's too perfect."

I smile wide up through my windshield, laughing at the timing of the drops and my incredible fortune. My soft top beats above from the pummeling rain. I blink, lashes flutter with each puff of sound. My cheeks awaken, remembering the soft waves of purple wings. I grab my phone. This is too important. I need to text Steve. My fingers move fast, high on the reclaimed beauty that signs do exist. I tell him about my painting, the butterflies, and my unburdened rock. I text him everything—a stream of words sent fearlessly because I know he'll understand. I stare at my phone. I reread the long blue block as the sending bar stops and takes too long. My message turns green. My heart stops. I stare at my frozen words, chest draining, disappearing fast, but then the ellipsis appears. I sigh. My service was bad. Way out here, I should have known. I watch the three dots pulse rhythmically across the bottom like a heart hooked up to a screen. The failed connection was only a false alarm.

"Fuck yeah! That's awesome. I'm having a great day too. Lots of crazy stuff. Can't wait to tell you about it."

I smile and breathe in, lungs filling fully. The rain softens. The drops pat like fingertips on my roof—warm pads tapping my skin. The three dots appear again. I watch them coolly this time.

"We should go camping again soon."

I keep the phone level as the water on my windshield drips together and snakes down. I travel along the stream—a snail trail, a fallen tear, amoebas collecting and slipping down. I don't know what I feel. Right now, I can't feel anything. I pull up the memories Steve captured and sent from our trip last October. He took all the pictures. He built the fire and bought all the beer. I came along and watched.

My finger stops on the sunset photo—his favorite picture but one I'm still trying to understand. Alone on the beach, I stood staring, looking off in the distance away from the sun. He said I looked beautiful, but my hands were shaking. My body hadn't adjusted yet to all the drugs.

Chapter Eleven

I take a sip of beer, pacing myself with a forkful of food in between to match the girls. The sweet, thick tang and smoked meat fills my loosening mind and draws me in. I steal several more quick bites and then push the plate aside. Rebecca's still eating, her glass full. The condensation collects at the bottom as she speaks effortlessly, but Katrina is like me. She hasn't even touched her food. We finish our drinks and look around, anxious for another.

"Rebecca, why aren't you drinking? Get on our level, girl!"

"I'm trying! You guys drink so fast."

"Lightweight." Katrina smirks and turns to me. "What are you getting?"

I know I should stick to beer, but my plan always fails. The buzz is too light. The bloat too disturbing beneath my dress.

"Vodka soda."

"Hell yeah! Melissa's awesome. I'm so happy you could make it out tonight."

I smile under her approval but quickly look down. I grab my glass of water to twirl the straw as I wait for my next drink. The waitress comes. We order.

Katrina continues, "You're so lucky you live here. I can't believe this is the first time we've gone out in Newport."

Rebecca laughs, mouth full. "Not my first time." She swallows and takes a sip of water. "You should've seen Melissa on Saint Patty's Day. I think she made out with the whole town."

My cheeks burn. The drinks come fast. I suck up the vodka, poisoning my tongue, numbing out the surfacing memories that only a blacked-out mind would understand.

"That's not gonna happen again. I don't care about boys. All I care about is being with the two of you."

Rebecca rolls her eyes. "Oh yeah, I forgot. You're doing that whole 'on your own' thing."

Her words sting. I press my feet deeper into my heels, but the stiletto stunts the ground and forces the pressure into my toes. I miss my counselor.

Rebecca raises her glass as if to take a sip. "Well, *I* personally am looking for some action tonight. Katrina, you with me?"

My face tightens, ready for the bold, loud words, but across from me, Katrina is quiet. I peek up. She's different. She's watching me, soft eyes and subtle verbs.

"I think it's cool what you're doing. I wish I could feel good on my own."

For a moment, I'm naked, caught in Katrina's milky twilight. I break the connection and shake the feeling away. Waves of vodka roll in. They coat heavily over my skin, sealing over my face like a welcomed mask.

"You can. Anyone can. Nobody here needs a guy."

Katrina nods, believing my staccato words, but Rebecca only laughs.

"Yeah, okay guys, do whatever you want, but I'm not spending the rest of my life alone. I've got needs, needs you girls can't fill."

They both laugh. I laugh too. The alcohol seeps down to a place we all understand. My thighs soften under sheets of warmth. My mind rolls over to picture a stranger, but even that fantasy is forever changed. I cross my legs and harden like stone, hating my primal side almost as much as I hate my heart.

"Even those needs you can fill on your own. I really enjoy masturbating."

Rebecca slurps down a solid inch of her drink, drowning out my words. Her newfound grip on the glass strangles away any timidity. "Mm, I still prefer the real thing. All right, ladies, are you ready to go?"

I straighten up and quickly finish my drink.

"Yes. Definitely. Where do you wanna go?"

Katrina perks up. "Somewhere where we can dance!"

I smile. I couldn't agree more, but Rebecca's on a different tempo.

"What about that bar we went to Saint Patty's Day with all the bearded guys? I wanna go there."

I swallow. My enthusiasm cools. "You mean Pantomime?"

"Yes! That was it. Can we go there first?"

My hands tremble in my lap. I squeeze them together, a knot blocking the space between my thighs.

"Sure."

"Awesome! Let's go."

We hobble along the cobblestone streets, sidewalks too crowded with loose jaws and swaying arms. I walk fast, but Rebecca and Katrina linger behind, leaning in to the watchful eyes.

"Heyy, ladies. Where are you headed?"

"I don't know. Why don't you come and find out?"

The alcohol has hit Katrina. I can tell by the thickening sass in her voice.

"You should come with us to Gotham. You girls look like you wanna dance."

"Maybe we will if you're lucky."

"Ooooh."

"All right, Katrina. Come on, let's go."

I step up onto the sidewalk, blazing a path through the stumbling swarm of melting people. Their eyes droop, bodies drip. I'm caught between repulsion and a desperate need to fit in. Blending in can be a disguise. Blending in can be a way to survive.

At the entrance to the bar, the bouncer stops me. I fumble for my card, head down, but it doesn't matter. He's already seen my face.

"You're the girl who walks dogs, right?"

I look up. "Yeah."

"You're all set."

I slip inside, underneath the cloak of the dark bar. My shoulders tense up as I stand alone, surrounded by secret eyes, bloodshot and burning all around. Irrational fears: I wish this was something I believed, but my body knows better. I breathe in as my friends join me on either side.

"This place is packed!"

"Yeah, it always is."

Our heels stick to the floor as we squeeze our way toward the bar. The wall of insatiable zombies stops my friends. I push through and look back.

"What do you guys want?"

"What are you getting?"

Bumped from the side, I catch myself on the arm of the girl beside me. She glances down. My voice is small. She elbows my apology away. I turn to my friends.

"I think I'm just gonna get a beer."

"A beer!"

I waver in the blast of disappointment. Katrina needs me—she needs someone to join her in going down, but Rebecca is sobering up. She's stiff and wary too.

"Yeah, a beer actually sounds good."

Katrina sighs. "Fine. I'll do the same."

The bartender spots me and looks down. Eyes averted, he walks over.

"What can I get you?"

"Three Yuenglings, please."

I grip the edge of the bar as he nods and pulls the tap. His arm works mindlessly—conditioned to be that way. I take the first glass and turn around, relieved and surprised my friends are still so near.

"Here you go, and here's the other..."

Rebecca smiles faintly. "Thanks, Melissa. I'll buy the next round."

"Woohoo! Let's go meet some boys!"

The confidence has shifted. Katrina leads as Rebecca and I follow her into the backroom. She hesitates as a careless hand raises a pointed dart.

"Excuse me, asshole!"

He turns and looks down.

"Whoa, didn't see you there, feisty."

"You see me now, bitch?"

I gulp a layer of beer and smile discretely. Rebecca falls to the back as we walk single file through the glass door onto the patio.

Outside, the air is laced with smoke and intoxicated babble. The hard tables and iron chairs are spilling with people sprawled too openly, laughing too loud, sweating too much. Katrina makes her way past a ping-pong game. She plows through the vacant spectators and sits on the stone wall.

Rebecca tucks herself beside on Katrina's left, so I sit down to guard her right. The lights are too bright—spotlights on my friends' bare thighs. I cross my legs and pull the bottom of my dress further down. A thin layer of black isn't enough. The predators stare, birthed by swallowed intentions, ignited in cadaver's eyes.

"Do you girls want to have one beer here and then go some-where else?"

Rebecca nods, but Katrina looks around. "Why? There are so many hot guys here!" She turns to Rebecca. "I thought you said you liked this place?"

"No, I do. It would just be fun to try some other places. Plus, Melissa, didn't you say you got kicked out of here once?"

A stray ping-pong ball hits my head. I try to laugh it off, but I'm too sober. My body burns under the heat of menacing eyes.

"Yeah, but it was for something really messed up. I blacked out."

Katrina nods and returns to her drink, but Rebecca won't let it go.

"Didn't you yell at an old woman or something?"

"An old woman!" Katrina chokes. "Oh my god, Melissa, why?"

I turn away from her wide eyes, hiding inside the rim of my glass. "I don't know, guys. It was stupid." My words drip down, echo-ing within the glass hole, muted in the depth of beer. I want to fall in, morph, transform, and slip to the bottom, forever a speck over-looked, too small to fear.

"Couldn't you see Melissa getting into a bar fight? I feel like she has a secret anger streak."

My head shoots up, eyes sharp and alert by Rebecca's claim. She's laughing. She's energized. She doesn't understand the pain caused by such flame.

"All right, guys, ready to leave?"

I stand up and chug down the rest of my beer. The taste is warm and flat. I hold in a bitter gag as I wait for my friends to do the same. They follow me through the crowd as I storm ahead out the front door. Back onto the street, my legs stop, arrested by a different fear. As they gather around, the booze finally sets in, stirring awake my own detestable eyes. Rebecca looks to me.

"Where do you want to go?"

The innocent question curls as it moves toward me. My desire slithers, crooked down my neck, widening and undulating through my waist.

"Let's go across the street."

"Are we gonna go dancing?"

"Yeah, but let's go this way first."

My hips roll as I lead them away from the noise. Packs of hungry mouths pass by, but I am a wolf among the dogs. I glare as they nip, parting the sea of soulless games in search of something far more precious.

Through the dim streetlight, I find my prize. I smile wide and sashay ahead, summoning a strong intoxication to mask the flutters underneath.

"Steve!"

His two dogs rush toward me, pulling at the leash, but I plow past and capture him in my arms. Nostrils flared, my head rolls into the primal smell. His biceps hang limp, tucked close, afraid and unaware that his natural scent is what I crave.

My eyes flash open. I back away quickly to blend in with my friends.

"Guys, this is Steve. Steve, these are my beautiful friends!"

He doesn't smile. He doesn't do anything. The light in his face is gone. I scratch my face and look down.

"All right, well, good to see you."

I glance up fast and then usher my friends away. Distance doesn't matter though. My heart feels what he feels. I try to escape forward, but my friends surround me like bees. Their questions prick, each one a painful sting.

"He's *hot*! How do you know him?"

"Why didn't you guys stay together?"

"Are you crazy? You should date him!"

My legs power forward, but everything above the shoulders grows small.

"I don't want to date anyone. I just want to be alone."

Their prying words continue to swarm. My mouth seals up, throat swollen to the allergic reaction. I close my eyes. Time skips forward to a drowned-out bar. The music is loud. All around, bodies undulate close and sweaty. Hands from behind hold my waist, stunting my rhythm, trying to control. I turn around and push the stranger aside, wading through the all-too-familiar sea. My bladder bulges. I crawl up the railing to the second floor. Katrina and Rebecca appear.

"Are you going to the bathroom?"

I nod, head heavy, chin rolling side to side.

"Oh, good! We wanna come too!"

My body waves, unstable on both sides. Boney arms slip under my own and carry me into the false light. My eyelids squeeze as I cringe. I find myself alone in a stall, phone in hand, desperate in the wake of an already-sent text. The three dots appear—dark spots across the screen like ancient blood. I squint to read Steve's response. The bold type punctures my chest and snaps back into the phone, leaving my rib cage open and bleeding.

Do you even like me when you're sober?

All senses crumble. The screen goes black as my insides empty. I flush the toilet but remain sitting. I'm stuck to the ceramic bowl.

"Melissa? Are you still in here?"

Rebecca's voice reaches through a crack—an angel's soft and delicate wing.

"Yeah, I'm coming."

The white feathers lift my body from the bathroom, out onto the street, up the hill, and back home. They leave me to sleep off the disease—sleep away the cavity that is deep and unknown.

Chapter Twelve

My mom wanders over to the trail entrance as I transfer my rocks from the old backpack into the new one. The rocks clop together. A molten mound bubbles up my esophagus, but I push it down.

"Thank you again, Mom. My old bag was starting to fall apart."

"Oh, you're welcome! I hope it's the right size."

I zipper the top and bend my knees to hoist the bag on. The tension squeezes up my gut—a shameful paste crawling up my throat like a slug.

"Do you need help putting it on?"

"No, I'm good."

The hip belt buckles around my rib cage. The breast strap clips and rubs my collarbone. I slide the top strap down as far as it'll go, but the hip belt can't be adjusted. Gravel shifts. My mom's footsteps near. I struggle fast to shift everything down.

"Let me see."

I force a smile and let go. The strap pops back up, framing and lifting my breasts. My cheeks burn. Her hands clasp together, brows sweet and soft.

"Aw, it looks like it's hugging you."

The rouge in my cheeks fades, but my chest continues to bulge. I walk ahead to lead the way, wishing I had worn a tighter bra.

"So you really do this every day?"

The path widens. I slow down to walk beside her.

"Yeah. Sorry, I know it's weird. Thanks for coming along."

"No problem! I think it's amazing. I don't know anyone else with your kind of discipline. You're like a monk!"

A rock imbedded in the path guides me to walk slightly ahead. I push the hip belt down again, but it's no use. Underneath the strap, my bloated belly protrudes, emphasized and exposed. On top, my chest bounces. I am a walking spectacle—shame twofold in the front, a pile of pain on my back. I breathe in.

"I don't have a choice. This is the backbone of my project."

"Well, just be careful. I know how you can be. I don't want you out here in the middle of a hurricane just because you think you *have* to be."

I step out from the shade into the bright meadow along the dirt path. Angled down, my hat's brim protects me. Coated on my upper lip and scar, the sunscreen shields me. Still, I feel a desire to run, afraid of the blinding rays.

"Mom, I walk outside for a living. I'll be fine."

"That's true." Her words mumble out behind me, sad and small. My legs grow weak. I slow to match her pace, cursing my temper—the way I always seem to push people away.

"Did you know you're the best mom ever?"

She smiles, head still down. My shoulders hunch. I shrink in her pain.

"I don't know any other mom who would love a daughter as crazy as me."

Her hand reaches out, soft on my arm. I want it to stay.

"You're not crazy. You're passionate as hell!" She laughs. "And stubborn as anything."

Relief bursts from my lips, saliva thick with snot from the sadness I'm conditioned to hold in. A hawk calls overhead. My mom and I look up. We watch it soar above the field.

"So your sister has really been enjoying the dinner dates with you!"

A cloud coats the sun. I shift the weight on my back, stomach grumbling and grotesque. The hunger pain isn't real. I'm clogged with the secret damage from last night. I want to believe I can change. I want to believe today is the day I finally escape this pattern.

"Me too. I'm glad we've found a healthy way to hang out."

I scratch my neck. My mom does the same.

"Yeah, it's pretty perfect. Nothing more wholesome than meeting up for a bite to eat! And I know your sister really appreciates it. Especially with everything that's been going on with Creg."

A crow caws from a branch ahead. We slip under the cool relief of the shadowed trees. The leaves above are a welcomed disguise. My voice comes out flat from a place buried deep and unfortunately real.

"I know."

"I just don't understand!" My mom's arms fly up—a shrill and desperate wave sent through the air. "I can't tell if he's lying or if the ex-girlfriend is crazy."

My head twitches. I clench my jaw to hold in the rising fury. "Yeah, who the fuck knows."

"I mean, she could be telling the truth. I never really liked Creg. I'm not sure why your sister thinks he's so wonderf—"

"To be honest, I fucking hate him." I rub my brow, the beading sweat, the stupid way my emotions can never be contained. "I think the whole situation is weird, and Man needs to get out. Ever since she met him three months ago or whatever it was, she's gotten weaker. That's not love. Love is supposed to make you feel—"

My head drops down. My body turns to stone. The dirt beneath my feet blurs and fades as I retreat inside. My mom dips her head down to stare, waiting for more, unaware that I am trapped in a pit, small and hidden, at the bottom of my rib cage where feelings don't exist.

"I'm trying to stay away from guys, all guys. The only person I want to date is myself."

"Oh? Okay. Yeah that sounds like a good plan. For a little while…"

"No, Mom. I'm serious. I don't want to date anyone else." I breathe in and lift my head as the path straightens. With the evergreens tall and evenly planted on either side, I am safe again to emerge. "This weekend, I'm actually planning to go back to Trumbull and take myself out to dinner. I'm gonna drop off the rock about Shamus there, but more so, I want to focus on enjoying myself. I might even get a hotel room."

"Are you gonna see Shamus while you're there?"

My mouth twitches. The muscles in my neck tense.

"No. That would defeat the whole purpose."

"Okay! I was just asking. I know you started talking to him again last summer, so I didn't know."

I close my eyes to breathe in deep. The wind picks up in my ears—cleansing waves across tall grass. I open to find myself in the meadow. My mom is still here. No time or space has passed.

"I did a lot of things last summer, Mom. I'm not that person anymore. I've moved on. I'm starting to heal."

She reaches her hand out toward my shoulder, light fingertips on the sleeve of my tee. The touch irritates—too gentle like a trickling stream. I curl away from her—away from the timidity—caving in closer to the sturdy new straps under my arms. Tears form. *What's wrong with me?* The question swirls, carrying along memories of my mom's face. She was so joyful when she first got here. She's always so joyful to see me.

"You *are* healing. Your father and I are so proud."

I look up to see the truth, but her eyes turn too quickly away.

"Not everyone has the guts to face their problems like you do."

Her words crumble out. She brushes her bottom lip and seals over the mess with a smile. I place my hand on her back. Her bones are weak. A flood pours out from my chest through my arm, pooling under my open hand. She doesn't react. Her frame remains small.

"Mom, did you know I think about you every time I come out here? Actually, every time I'm in the woods?"

"Aw, you're so sweet."

"No, it's true! Remember when you used to take me and Man hiking when we were kids?"

Her cheeks glow. "Yes. That was so fun."

I gaze ahead into the memories: the wet rock under my hands, the way my mom used to let me climb, clamber, and score up the cliffs into the branches and high up the trees. She wasn't afraid. She was proud. She used to climb too.

"Oh wow, there's the parking lot!"

My eyes fade back in. "You're right. That went by fast."

"It did! It was kinda fun too. I mean, I know I'm not carrying rocks like you, but the hike itself was very pleasant."

I open the passenger door and unclip the bag. "Good. I'm glad you had a good time."

I grab my phone from the floor and scroll through as I walk around the other side. No messages. Through the window, my mom sits with her head down, smiling, glued to the screen in her hand. Her fingers tap lightly, typing back to faceless mysteries—ones I've learned from adolescence I'd rather not understand. I breathe in, chest tight, retreating to my own secrets—the drunken pleas from another blacked-out night and Steve's words.

"No, Melissa. I'm sorry, but it's not a good time."

I back out and delete the convo—a pitiful attempt to erase the shame. I get in and start up the car. My mom buzzes as I drive. Her mouth moves like a puppet—a marionette passing along someone else's words, hyped by the gossip, intrigued and elated along the grapevine's twisted ways. My face tightens, all muscles restrained.

"Oh, by the way, how did you like the new backpack?"

I breathe in. I want to lie. I want to be cool. I want to be grateful, but my jaw is locked up. Only true words can escape.

"Mom, I gotta be honest. It's too small."

"Oh no! I thought it looked good on you."

I turn away, eyes sharp and ashamed. My voice comes out small.

"It's made for a child."

Chapter Thirteen

The sun warms my back as the breeze blows gently, carrying green-tinted giggles from the two middle-aged women beside me. I keep my eyes on my book as I grip the next page, bending the corner, smiling as I pretend to not be listening. The sweet smoke curls in the air. The women laugh again, past the point of remembering to blow in the other direction. Their delight blooms across the small beach. Mine tingles secretly inside. I've never felt so independent before. I thought I would feel sad, but returning to Trumbull feels much more like a solo vacation than a day of mourning. Shamus has barely been on my mind.

I flip the page even though the sentence doesn't interest me. Beyond my book, above the stone steps, my Jeep stands proud, parked beside the women's van beneath the shade of the tall pines. I wink at the round headlights. Everything feels alive today. Newport feels far away. The whispers and discomfort are contained, miles down the highway in a forgotten world. I smile at the masculine edges of my Jeep's frame—its strong front wheels and sturdy stance. A flurry of charged warmth fills my chest. I pat the flowered bandeau around my head and return to my book as the chairs fold and a blanket shakes out next to me. As the women pack up and leave, I wait on the page. Their van backs up and pulls away, leaving the lot, the beach, and the pool of fresh silent water behind me. I turn over and breathe.

The floating dock in the middle tempts me out, but the sun feels too good on my skin. I run my hands over my smooth warm legs and survey the lake's sparkling surface. Voices from hidden shores echo across the water, distant and disguised somewhere within the perimeter of trees. The sounds are comforting like a pleasant lingering dream. I sigh and breathe in as the wind lifts the ends of my ponytail toward the evergreen nearest me. The tall trunk and delicate tickle on my neck sparks a memory: thirty tea-lights illuminated and glued to a large whiteboard in the shape of a heart. My palm opens to cup a hand from the past.

Shamus brought me here when I was fifteen. We were celebrating Valentine's Day.

His invisible hand in mine is young and bold. It lifts me to my feet and leads me down the sand. I pull my hair free from the elastic and toss it aside as I step into the lake. I walk until the water is high enough to wade, and then my head leans back, hair like weeds in the current. The sun showers over my face.

Laughing, I doggy paddle around. I know other ways to swim, but this juvenile one is still my favorite. I head in the direction of the dock beyond where my feet can touch. The ladder is close, but suddenly, the depth grows cold. Thoughts of eyes and untamed growth creep up from the dark. I turn around and swim back to shore. On the blanket, my hair drips down my spine, darkening the cloth.

I take the folded towel and wrap it around my body. With my bare skin covered, I look back at the water and shake my head. *Childish.* The dock isn't far out. The ladder seems so accessible from here. A small nudge from behind dares me to try again, but I pull up my knees and secure the towel tighter around. The wind blows. My hair is drenched and cold.

As my body dries and the sun sinks down, a different kind of shiver sets in. *Dining alone.* I can't avoid it. I promised myself I would do it, but I have been dreading the idea all day. Logic says I'm being ridiculous. Logic knows people go out to dinner by themselves all the time, but still, I cower. My left palm opens to search for the invisible hand, but the sound of tire over gravel disrupts the illusion. A white Subaru rumbles to park behind me.

"Of course."

I slip on my dress and pack up to leave, tossing the blanket and towel in the back seat. Through the window, a boy leads a girl out of the car. I start up my Jeep and back out of the lot, escaping before the couple can settle on the sand.

In town, I stop for gas even though my tank is half full. The streetlights click on. I look around. My thumb taps the pump as a pack of black-hooded kids skate down the sidewalk, their hard rubber wheels grind the pavement. I flatten the ends of my dress as they near closer. I can hear the tinny sound of music as they roll by, full-volume blasting from their headphones. Their baggy clothes flap in the wind, creating their own draft. I squint to read the back of their sweatshirts. I recognize every band. My chest opens, reaching out suddenly, desperate to catch up with them, but the longing is all internal. The gas guzzles to the top, and the pump clicks. I pay and get back on the road. The sidewalks are empty. The kids must have disappeared around a building. I drift around. I could leave Trumbull early. The easy out tempts my mind. I could drop off my rock fast, grab food on the way home, and pretend to be proud, but a car beeps suddenly. I speed around. I swerve and pull off the road, braking too fast. My duffel bag falls to the floor.

Eyes wide, I park and unstick my grip from the steering wheel. I breathe in as I pull the duffel bag back onto the seat, straining at the forgotten weight—the forgotten smile I had all morning as I stuffed extra shoes and extra clothes inside. I was so elated—so optimistic by the thought of adventure. *Where has that energy gone?* I place my hand on the zipper, remembering the pajamas and toothbrush I packed just in case. I was brave this morning. I was open to all possibilities.

I place one hand back on the steering wheel and shift into drive. "We've got to do this, self. We promised." I push down on the pedal to pick up speed. The engine roars through me, awakening a deeper tone—a voice I haven't heard in a while. I smile. "Time to grow a pair and take myself out on a date."

I pull up the hill in the adjacent town and park in a dark corner beside a strip mall. Quickly, I change out of my suit and ease into some fresh dry clothes. I suck in. The button on the white shorts is tight, but my black top flows over, disguising the rolls. I check my face in the mirror and step out. As I approach the neon sign, I rehearse the line burning in my head: *table for one, table for one.* The palm trees lining the front door guide me in. Three hosts stand, waiting to greet me. I burst toward them.

"Table for one!"

All three jump. They scramble for a menu as I look away and clear my throat. I contain a smile as the least frightened one leads me into the dining room, motioning toward a two-top, kitty-cornered between a wall and an opaque divider. The fear and embarrassment cools.

"Okay for you?"

"Yes! This is perfect."

I slide in on the booth side, placing my purse next to me to seal off the open space. I breathe in, cozy and safe.

"Something to drink?"

"Yes, please. A mai tai."

He nods fast and walks away, opening my view to the room. The corner of my mouth curls. *What was I so afraid of?* By the far window, a young couple sits, enwrapped in their own world. Through the divider's clouded glass, a man drinks alone at the bar. Everywhere else, the tables are empty. I pull out my phone to check the time—7:15 p.m. Perhaps the sushi isn't as good as I remember.

"Mai tai."

I zipper my phone back up and push the purse aside. The waiter sets my drink down and looks to the untouched menu in the center of the table. I pick it up. I already know what I want.

"Can I have the ginger salad and paradise roll?"

"Anything else?"

"Mm." I take a sip of my mai tai. "Yeah. I'll also get the coconut soup."

He scribbles down my order and takes the menu. Once alone again, I lean back with the straw to my lips. The fruity liquid awakens my taste buds, exciting my tongue tangy and sweet. As the cool juice coats my throat, its potency warms open my chest. I sigh and smile easily. The fuzzy comfort expands beyond my rib cage, sprinkling down like warm sand on a beach. I wiggle my toes. I never knew being alone could feel so good.

The waiter returns with all three dishes in his hand. I put my drink aside and move the utensils and centerpiece. He arranges the dishes. My cheeks burn. There's just enough room on the table.

"Anything else?"

I laugh. "No, I think I'll be set for a while."

He hesitates and then walks away. Over by the window, the girl looks over. I look down. I need to eat slow. Eyes on the bowl, I spoon up the soup. The sweet milk is lukewarm. I wish it were hot.

The waiter returns on my last slurp of broth.

"Another mai tai?"

I swallow and put the spoon down. He takes away the empty dish and stares. I look to the glass.

"Uh…"

I know I shouldn't. I know what I need to say. Still, the ice cubes melt into the last inch of my drink, watering down the vibrancy pale pink. I suck up the remaining sip and hand him the glass.

"Okay."

He nods and walks away. I reach for my salad and force the fork down. The corners of the room blur, wavy and malleable in the distance where the couple sit. I gaze, secure within my liquid armor as time shifts, and their faces change. Me and Shamus. We were celebrating our four-year anniversary. In ghostly form, we are celebrating again. Not old enough to drink, the waitress sets down a root beer and a diet coke. We clink glasses and smile. My younger self turns, but she doesn't see me. I stare at her rounded cheek, willing the curtain of hair to flow aside and open toward me. *Would she be proud? Would she squint and see someone she might hope to be?*

The waiter interrupts with my second mai tai.

"Thank you."

Without responding, he disappears around the corner as I reach for the glass. With each gulp, the liquid sunrise spreads warmth through my veins. I could close my eyes. I could slurp up every last drop of nectar, but I stop myself halfway and pull out my phone instead. The names in my contact list roll up easily, blurring together in a stream of tempting numbers. The warmth reaches the tips of my fingers. My nail beds glow. The yearning is strong. I want to open up and click every name. Suddenly I miss everyone.

I take a picture of my salad and compromise, texting only my sister.

First time dining alone!

I put my phone away and look around. The couple by the window has left. Two other pairs have been seated. I take another sip of my drink and stab the bunches of lettuce, chewing fast through the wilted pieces. The sent message repeats in my head, sounding dumb. I finish the salad and swap plates, immediately stuffing in my next bite. The sushi from my memories tasted sweet—hints of banana and mango mixed with lobster—but everything right now sort of tastes the same. I stuff in another mouthful of packed rice. The large clumps fill my throat. Eyes glazing over, there is no need to pause. I eat until there's nothing left, and then I suck up the rest of my drink, tilting the glass to slurp the airy drops between the ice.

"Anything else?"

Head heavy, my gaze rolls up. I smile, cheeks swollen.

"Just the check, please."

The empty plates slip away, revealing darkened spots where the soy sauce dripped and bled through the cloth. I look across the tainted white to the chair pushed all the way in. No space for a body. I slide down, tugging the top of my shorts to make room for my bloated waist. The dining room swirls. I can't tell if the eyes staring are conjured or real. I can't tell if they're sad or intrigued. I stretch my toes under the table and push at the legs of the empty chair. The space opens a few inches, but still, I can't imagine anyone in the seat. This was supposed to feel like a date. This meal was supposed to be empowering, but there are two stories, at least: one about a girl learning to love herself and be on her own, and one about a girl haunting her ex-boyfriend's town. Lost in the spilled brown spots, the eyes continue to stare. I don't know which story I believe. I don't know which one everybody else sees.

The check comes, and I fill it with cash. I grab my purse and stand up to leave, but the floor moves. I touch the opaque wall as I round the corner and steady myself.

"Have a good night!"

I glance back and wave before slipping out the door. In my car, I climb inside and unbutton my shorts, reclining the seat as my belly shifts. I cradle the pressure mound underneath with one hand. I shouldn't have ordered so much food. I shouldn't have had two drinks. I unzip my purse and search for my phone. The bright screen wobbles in my hand. I ease the light and wait for my eyes to focus. No messages. Unobstructed, the time shines clear. My thumb browses for hotels, sloppily and fast. I swipe through the options, reading the occasional word, aware I'm only stalling. I don't want to stay here, but I'm not sober enough to go home. A familiar image flashes by on the screen. I slide back up and click the hotel. It's the one where Shamus and I stayed—the one we got earlier this year.

I place the phone on my belly and pinch the inner ducts of my eyes. I haven't completed my plan. I haven't finished what I came here to do. My stomach sloshes as I flip over and reach under the seat. I dig into my backpack and pull out the rock on top. I know where I want to leave it. I just don't remember how to get there.

I ease my seat upright and stare at the phone. I don't even need to search my contacts. I've had Shamus's number memorized since I was thirteen. My thumb hovers over the screen, caught between my mom's words and my own condescending voice: *Are you going to see Shamus?* I scratch my chin but quickly stop. I dial the number and hold up the phone. Shamus picks up on the second ring.

"*Hellooo*…haven't heard from you in a while…"

I button my shorts and sit up. "I know, but that's not why I'm calling. I have sort of a strange question."

"Uh-oh. Okay. What is it?"

"No, it's nothing bad. Just random. Do you, uh, remember the quarry we went to when we were kids?"

"You mean the gravel pile we climbed back in high school?"

My eyes widen. "Yes! Oh my god. I can't believe you remember."

"Yeah, of course I do. We talked about aliens and saw a bunch of shooting stars."

"Yes! Do you know where that place is?"

He laughs. "Yeah, but it doesn't exist anymore. Fuckers turned it into a Home Depot parking lot."

"What?" My voice cracks. The beam of light flickers and fades in my eyes.

"Yeah, it sucks. I tried going back there a few years ago, and that's when I found out." He pauses. "Why do you ask? Are you in town?"

My breath stops. I know I should lie. My mind spins, in search of a cover-up, but my lips are loose. I tell him everything.

"No way! Dude, why didn't you call me? We could've hung out all day."

My mouth closes. He continues, "I'm eating right now, but I'm literally five minutes down the road from you. When I'm done, we should meet up!"

My smile curls in the dark. "Okay."

"Sweet! I'll call you when I'm leaving."

He hangs up, and the world goes silent. I try to sit with the emptiness—allow the dark space to wash over me like the cool lake water, but my ears start to ring. I twist out the stupid smile on my face and start up my car. I don't care what Shamus says. I don't care if the quarry has been demolished. I still need to go and see for myself.

Following the GPS to the nearest Home Depot, I cross back into Trumbull, hugging the turns. The streetlights guide me. I pass under their soft spots—beacons leading me through the dark. A paved opening splits the trees to my right and pulls me up a hill. I drive slow, hesitant because I recognize everything, and the voice from my GPS tells me I'm about to arrive.

At the very top, the truth spreads wide. The mountains of rock and sand have all been flattened, paved and painted over with even lines. I drive around aimlessly, floating like a shade in a cemetery. As I near the far end, the long concrete building grows undeniably real. I drift around the back, away from the bright entrance lights, desperate to see the stars. My windshield is clouded. I park and step out, angry by the dumpster, the discarded wooden pallets, and the film coating the sky. I walk to the edge of the trees with the rock ready in my hand, but out of the darkness, a small mountain materializes. I breathe in the warm mulch.

With one hand grasping the rock, I attempt the ascent. My flip-flops sink as I fall forward, struggling to keep my white shorts clean and my toes free of dirt. I step and fall again, but this time, I laugh. *Who cares?* I kick off my sandals and crawl to the top. Booze-driven or inspired by something else, I reach the summit and sink down, allowing the soft shavings to mold around my seated body. I smile as I dig up the mulch and bury my feet under its dark red color. My toes wiggle, delighted and warm.

I look up at the tree line and the twinkling city lights down below. I could stay here forever. The view is different than I remember, but the beauty still exists. Suddenly though, a buzzing sound fills my ear. I slap the mosquito away and scratch the disturbance, trying to return to the view, but the high-pitched wings and dangling legs start to swarm. I flail my arms around and stand up quickly. There is no time to think. I chuck the rock as hard as I can into the trees. A branch snaps. The brush and leaves stir as the rock tumbles, and I clamber down. I collect my shoes and hurry into the car. Without brushing off my shorts or checking my phone, I drive. I make my way down the hill and back out to 95. I merge onto the highway as my phone rings.

"Hello?"

"Hey! I just finished dinner. Where are you?"

"Hey…I'm actually headed home."

"What?" He laughs. "You know, I kinda had a feeling."

The exit sign passes by slow. I drift on, remaining silent despite the change in his tone.

"Are you still mad at me?"

"Shamus, I was never mad at you. I was hurt. But believe me, I get it. We were both in a shitty place."

"Yeah." He pauses. His voice lowers, a deep whisper in my ear. "It was fun though…before Christina called."

"Stop! Don't do that!"

"Do what?"

"Treat me like a sex object. I'm a fucking person! You used to care. You used to be so different."

"I do care! I just…well, you know."

"Yeah. You're miserable in your relationship, so you use me. Fuck you."

"Hey! Come on. You know me. Don't do that thing you always do."

"What? Stand up for myself?"

He sighs. "Look, I get it. I fucked up, but I'm not the enemy."

My chest is tight. I look back over my shoulder and move into the left lane.

"You always get so mad." He laughs. "People make mistakes. I felt bad when you had me come to Newport and meet Steve."

"Why? He and I weren't dating."

"Yeah, but he *really* liked you." He laughs nervously. "And okay, don't get mad, but you kinda acted like an asshole that night."

I scratch my face. "I know. I know. I got too drunk."

"Well, not only that, but you kept talking about how great I am right in front of him. I really liked Steve."

I cringe and pull the receiver away from my ear. The air is sharp—painful pricks against the lining of my lungs. I breathe in slow, trying to make room.

"I had just gotten out of the hospital. I was confused."

"I know." His voice is soft. "And Christina and I were in a bad place. I was confused too."

My cheek leans in to the phone. The needle pricks fade away. I sink heavy but in a comforting, puddling sort of way. The muscles in my body let go.

"Hurt people hurt people." The truth mutters out.

"And horny people horn people."

I laugh. "Shamus, shut up."

We stay on the phone as I make my way home. The conversation delves and changes wildly, the way it used to when we were kids. I've missed this type of flow—spontaneous and light yet continuously drawn into the deep. I remember now why I used to love staying up with him on the phone. Time and distance disappears. Suddenly, I'm approaching Pell Bridge.

"Oh shit, Shamus, I've actually gotta go. I'm almost home."

"Aw, man. That was fast."

"I know, right? Those two hours flew by."

"They did!" He pauses. "Dude, it was really nice talking to you."

"You too." I laugh. "Definitely not how I planned to end today, but that's okay. I guess it's what we needed."

"Yeah, don't ever ex me out, you psycho."

I smile. "Have a good night."

I place the phone aside and float over the bridge. Up high, Newport is beautiful. The decorated boats and illuminated harbor never loses its charm. I descend and take the first exit off the bridge, holding my breath as I merge onto Farewell Street. There are other turns—longer routes I could take to get back home—but I continue straight through the dark neighborhood. Just before the hill to my apartment, I slow and look around. I check every corner, squinting at the distant cars, searching for the parked white Subaru—Steve's white Subaru. I wish I didn't have to look. I wish I could drive by and not care.

Chapter Fourteen

Where are you, Miss?

I text back quickly and then flip over my phone. The old man smiles beside me and sips his drink. He can see me clearly. He knows I'm not like most people my age.

"Meeting someone here?"

I grab my mojito. "Yeah, my sister. Not my original plan, but she needs me."

He nods and breathes in. "What's your name?"

"Melissa. What's yours?"

"Bob." He holds out his hand. We shake—two surprisingly similar grasps. I put the drink down as my nerves steady. He reminds me of someone.

"What was your original plan, Melissa?"

My gaze drops down. I fiddle with the snake ring on my left hand. The metal is cheap. The head and tail wrapped around bend easily.

"Lately, I've been trying to do stuff on my own. Last night, I went to the movies by myself, and today, I wanted to have a drink at a bar for the first time alone."

"That's very interesting. What spurred on this drive to be alone?"

My fingers stop. I cover the snake. "I don't know. It's just something I need to do."

He breathes in slow, filling my own worn and tattered lungs. "I used to dream of sailing away. My wife never liked the water, but I always did."

I look up and follow his distant gaze. Behind me, the sun slips down in full bloom. The petals of light reach, spreading fire in the sky. We watch silently as the red fades to blue.

"Miss! There you are!"

The electricity shocks us both. The old man turns away as my sister barges between and sits down.

"Oh my god, you would not *believe* the traffic I had to get through. I'm so happy to finally be here with my *Missssss!*"

Her embrace engulfs. I take a long sip of my drink and widen my eyes. She sits down. I try to look bigger.

"Me too, Man. I'm glad you're here."

"Ugh. Worst day ever. I *need* a drink. Excuse me, sir? Hi, yes, I would like a shot of tequila and your strongest drink."

The bartender blinks but gains composure fast.

"Our signature cocktail, the Zombie, has several types of light and dark rum mixed with—"

"Yep! Sounds good to me."

He wavers for a moment, mouth still parted before walking away. My sister sighs and leans back to shake out her hair. Bob peeks up from his drink to look at me.

"Man, this is Bob. Bob, this is my sister, Amanda."

She whips around. "Oh, hi. Were you talking to my little sister while she was waiting for me?"

Her body is charged, blind and confused. Bob inhales and grows tall. The lines in his face harden into wood. He studies her like a totem pole, looking down.

"My sister just broke up with her boyfriend. She's having a bad day."

His eyes shift to me. He breathes in my desperate cues and shifts back.

"Your sister, Melissa, is a wonderful person."

"Yeah. I know."

Her sharp voice stings through his shroud. His eyes cloud as he crumbles away. My sister turns back to me and takes over the space.

"So, I finally fucking did it. Miss, you were so right about him. Thank *god*, I listened to you and cut him off."

My vision trembles from a hidden, internal blow. I spring away from the pain and return to the surface of my skin.

"I'm glad you feel that way. He really didn't deserve you."

Her drinks come. She tosses back the shot, gullet open wide. The whole patio shakes as she slams the glass down. I tremble but stare, intrigued by her power.

"You're the best, Miss. I really don't know what I would have done today without you."

My mouth twists as I look down.

"Yeah, I've learned it's important to ask for help. Some things are too hard to handle on your own."

"Mhm! And Mom and Dad would have just drove me crazy. I'm glad I left before either of them got home."

My phone dings. I reach out fast to shut off the sound.

"Sorry! I had the volume on for you. It's off now. I'm listening."

"No, Miss, it's okay." She laughs suddenly. "You should check actually. It might be Mom in a panic, wondering where I am."

I look down at the message, holding my breath. The disap-pointment flows. I lie to myself and pretend the feeling is relief.

"It's Erin. She wants to meet up for dinner. I'll tell her I'm busy—"

"No! I love Erin! Tell her to come. The more female support, the better."

I swallow and text back, doing as she says. The borders of my body disappear as my insides grow weak and small. I drink to feel in control. I drink to deny the truth. I slurp up the bottom and order another, pretending I'm not just a pawn moving from space to space in someone else's world.

Under the darkened sky, Erin arrives. We take our drinks and move to a table inside.

"So, Man, how are you? I haven't seen you in forever!"

The nickname rolls off Erin's tongue as naturally as it does off mine. I fiddle with my napkin. My sister leans in.

"Well, to be honest, I've been better. I think I'm still in shock. I broke up with that guy I was seeing today."

"Oh no! What did he do?"

My sister looks at me. "Miss knows everything. She helped me immensely today."

My shoulders lift, raised by her approval. I place a soft hand on her back and absorb the pain. I speak so she doesn't have to. I speak and explain, using only the words her body tells me to use.

"What a piece of shit! Fuck that guy. You're better off without him."

Erin raises her glass to cheer, but my sister's head is down. I know where she is. No amount of drugs or denial can save her from that place. I move close to whisper gentle truths in her ear, forgetting my own blood—the fiery blood that my sister and I both share. She swats me away.

"Everybody thought we were going to get married! I thought he was the one!"

The shock wave stuns the room. Silence ensues. Erin stares for a moment and then sips from her glass. I remain frozen, looking around from a shallow body out at all the afraid and shallow hearts. I wish I could cloak my sister and take her away—take her somewhere safe and warm where people understand.

"I'm sorry, guys. I need another drink."

"Yes! Good idea." Erin perks up. "Excuse me, sir, can we get the lady another drink?"

I breathe in and lean away as the waiter returns with a fresh round. We all suck up the toxins. Erin slows and savors the straw as the night and food go on, but I stay with my sister. Together, we always drown.

"Do you ladies want to wrap anything up?"

"Yes!" My sister and Erin laugh at the same time. Somehow, I've fallen out of sync. I poke at the ice in my glass as the energy continues without me. Cornered between them, I am small. Their waves are bright—vibrant and airy on a level I've never belonged. The waiter returns with the plastic containers. I grab them like a raft. I fork the rice in, one slow scoop at a time, stalling my inevitable sinking mind.

"Um, I'm sorry, but what the fuck are you doing?"

My chest turns to ice. The cold fills my ears as my sister's words swirl around. I peek up. They're both staring. They're both looking down.

"Jesus, let me do it."

Her hand snatches the container away. They both laugh. I watch from a hollow body as she and Erin mix together, boiling fast. They pack the rice and the rest of the food in, smiles manic, chattering jaws. The ridicules spray like spit in the air. From the depth inside, I can still feel their saliva.

The bill comes, and we pay. I get up to leave. Erin hugs us both goodbye, but I feel nothing. She asks if we can hang out again soon, but I only nod. She drifts away. I walk my sister to her car. She wobbles and gets in.

"I'll follow you!"

"Okay. I'll drive slow."

I float to my car. I float with the ghost inside, buried within. The door shuts. The silence rings, heavy in my ears, but I don't have the energy to cover the sound. I start up the car and head out, one eye to the rearview mirror, watching my sister behind. Her headlights swerve. They move in and out. I ease off the gas pedal, desperate to keep her in line. Desperate and jaded. Desperate and somehow already near the point of giving up. She and I are different. I wish we weren't, but for some reason, she never seems to learn.

At my apartment, I lead her up the stairs. She drops her purse and oversized duffel bag on the couch.

"Oh my god, I forgot how cute your apartment is!"

Her voice booms. Platform wedges against wooden floor, she pounds around. I watch her wander to the fridge—bottles and containers clink and shuffle around. Her bag falls over. Makeup and clothes spill out. I pretend not to care as a knot inside me twists, and my hands clench, knuckles popping.

"Miss, you have like nothing in your fridge!"

"What do you mean?"

"No mixers or anything to chase with." The freezer pops open. "Whoa! But you have tons of vodka."

I look to the clock and lie down. "There's seltzer water and lime juice on the bottom shelf. That should mix fine."

More suction as the fridge door bursts open and bangs against the wall.

"Oh, you're right! Okay, yes. That'll work."

I turn on the TV and turn up the sound. I choose a song she likes—a music video to remind her of happier times. The melody hits her like a drug. Ice cracks and falls on the kitchen floor. Stimulated veins, she rushes in.

"Yessss! Hell yeah, Miss. This is exactly what I need."

I try to absorb the warmth, but all I feel is sad.

"Good. Yeah, we can listen to whatever you want."

"Yes! More of this." She disappears and returns with two drinks. She always does. I take the glass and mask the jitters with a weak smile.

"Thank you, Man."

"Of course! Anything for my Miss."

I hand her the remote and sink down into the cushion, giving into my role. The videos on the screen stream by. The sound, the vodka, my sister's voice all blur together in a faraway, familiar past. I drink as a sacrifice. I drink to deny a pattern. I drink to avoid my own surfacing pain—the pain that I am, and always will be, used and alone.

"Ready for another?"

My sister squints and puckers her face, already three drinks in.

"No, Man, I'm all set. I gotta work in the morning."

Her head wobbles as she glares at my half-full glass. She grunts and gets up. Liquid spills—more ice hits the floor.

"Oops."

A cabinet opens. Yanked fast, she pulls out a drawer. She stumbles back in and pauses for a moment, gazing around. Her eyes sweep past, dark and drooped over me. She can't see. My sister is no longer around. Her body is fully possessed.

"Come on, Man. Let's go to bed."

I move toward her to guide her by the arm, but she pushes me down. I breathe in sharp, summoning a thick shield to try again.

"Man, I'm serious. It's time for bed."

She squeezes me in her eyes, pupils sharp like slivers. I soften and nod, remembering our differences—remembering the type of voice she needs.

"Come on, lovebug. I'll tuck you in."

Her jaw relaxes as her head lifts. She gives in to my motherly hand. I take her into the spare room and help her change out of her clothes.

"Do you want water?"

She moans and rolls aside. I scratch my neck, wishing I didn't understand. I ease the door shut as she begins to snore, leaving her to rest as I return to the kitchen. My eyes widen, but I feel no shock. Like a crime scene, her pain bleeds—it bleeds without her through melted cubes, broken glass, and empty bottles on the floor. I mop and sweep and clean up everything. On hands and knees, I make it all disappear as if it never happened—as if my own heart didn't break just the same and get taken away less than a year ago.

Chapter Fifteen

"What are you thinking about?"

My eyes lift from the carpet, but my body lies below lost in the fabric loops. "I had a rage dream last night."

"A what?"

My head falls back down. The room is heavy—underwater. My mouth moves slow. "A rage dream. That's what I call them. They've been happening since I was fifteen."

"And what are they about?"

Through blurred, vacant eyes, my mind drains to the floor. The sour stench follows. My sheets are still wet. The cold sweat permeates against time and space, reality and sleep, returning always with the same ferocity.

"My sister. My sister stealing and fucking a boy right in front of me."

The truth stings. I've never told anyone. I squeeze my eyes as my ears begin to ring. My thighs clench. In the tightened space, my fist balls up, desperate to beat. The pain wasn't enough this morning. It never is. Knives, scissors, and mallets lull. The dark crevice craves mutilation. It craves anything to take away the guilt of hating so intensely.

"That's interesting." My counselor leans back and breathes in. "Well, as long as you stay on your pills, you don't have to worry about those dreams coming true."

My nails dig deep into my skin. She doesn't get it. She didn't give me a chance to explain.

"So what else is going on? Are you still painting rocks?"

My claw retracts from my arm. "No." I breathe in and sigh, watching my anger drip down the wall. The blood pools and spreads across the radiator, but through the tainted air, my counselor still smiles—gentle, open, and reliably calm. The crimson fades soft pink. "The painted rocks are actually part of a larger project I'm working on. I've moved on to step two."

Her brows raise. "Really?" She grabs her tea and leans in. "Tell me more."

I look down to cross my legs. My finger traces circles in my hand. "I'm kind of trying to keep it a secret. I don't think anyone will understand."

Her warmth retreats but only for a moment to place down her tea. Her voice soothes and reaches for me. "I'm here. I'm listening."

I look up and absorb the sincerity in her eyes. My throat relaxes. I tell her everything—every detail of my plan. Her jaw drops, head shakes, glimmers of delight glow through her skin.

"That's...incredible!" She smiles, mouth open wide—a face of hers I've never seen before. "And you came up with this idea all on your own?"

"Yeah." I suppress a bubbling smile. "It all just sort of hit me one day."

"Wow! You are...to be honest, I'm amazed." She breathes in as her hands slide up her knees. "Okay, so you're done with step one, and now you're carrying the bigger rocks. How often do you carry them?"

"Every day. Well, pretty much. Not on weekends, but Monday through Friday, I have to carry them for at least an hour. It's my rule."

"How do you have time to do this? I mean, with your business and all?"

"I make time. Usually, I go after work, but today, I hiked early. I was out there at 6:00 a.m."

I look away for a moment, returning to the mist in the trees. Like the dew on the grass, the hairs on my arm shimmer moist. The rage disappears. Far from society, awakened by the rising tangerine light and the jungle sounds of morning birds, I am at peace. I breathe in. The walls and ceiling box me back in.

"It's actually my favorite part of the day. I wish I never had to leave the woods."

She cocks her head, cheeks drawn and suddenly sad. My eyes fall.

"I wanna try something with you. Have you ever done a body walk-through?"

I nibble the inside of my lip and shake my head. She breathes in.

"Okay, let's try it out. First, I want you to breathe deep and close your eyes. Try to relax. With each breath, let go of the tension in your body."

The air is shallow. I swallow and try again. Through my nose, the flood pours in. The dark behind my lids expands and grows depth with each exhale, pulling my consciousness out into space—a world free of boundaries and limitations.

"Listen to my voice. I am your guide on this journey. You are safe with me."

The warm words come from nowhere and yet echo all around. I drift comfortably, blanketed by this larger belief.

"Feel your toes. Feel your feet relax. Let the warmth coat up from the ground."

I look down. From the dark, my legs materialize and gravitate up. I pull my knees in and begin to spin. This isn't my body. The thighs are too thin.

"How do you feel?"

The spinning slows. The voice comes in satellite rings, green and soft, steadying me to an easier rotation.

"Sad. And small."

A tear forms. The rings flatten and grow wings. The voice is soft now, a delicate butterfly whispering in my ears.

"Melissa, you are not small. You have never been small."

My head bows. Like leaves in the breeze, the words swirl in. More tears. I soften my lids and let them fall.

"Melissa, the world does not need you to be small. The world wants you to be tall. Stand tall."

A hole inside fills. I release my legs as my back straightens. Saturated skin, my shoulders begin to rise.

"Stand tall. Stand tall."

Extended and long, my consciousness absorbs back. I open my eyes. My counselor is watching. She was watching the whole time.

"How do you feel now?"

I breathe in. "Better...oddly calm."

She smiles. My chest expands.

"I'm so glad. You're a beautiful person. You deserve calm."

She holds me in this strange truth—this foreign afterglow until the reflection is real. She gets up and moves to the bookcase by her desk. My eyes follow like a child in need—a child desperate to hold on and never lose this unconditional type of love.

"Here, I have something for you."

She grabs a crystal from her shelf and places it in my palm. I flip the soft pink over, rubbing my thumb along its opaque, flat edge.

"What is it?"

"Rose quartz. I want you to have it."

The crystal shifts naturally as my left hand squeezes around.

"Thank you. For everything today."

"You're welcome." She guides me to my feet and holds me in her arms. "You're a strong woman. Keep it up."

Chapter Sixteen

After my hike, I drive past my street and continue on along Bellevue toward Ocean Drive. Tourists crowd the sidewalks, drawn together like ants clustered around the mansions. I try to see what they see—I want to feel the excitement they feel—but the concrete giants drift by in the distance, flat and lifeless like a painted background.

At the crosswalk ahead, a family waits, so I slow down. I watch them smile and stroll by. I sink low in my seat as their voices invade my open window. I slip past the next approaching crowd and glide around the curve at the end of the street. As the sidewalks disappear and the mansions fade, I breathe. Along the winding road, I float with my foot resting on the pedal and my chest open, absorbing the cool breeze and the waves' rhythmic sound.

Leaning deep into the pavement's ebb and flow, my body remembers. I haven't been here in months, but even with my eyes shut, I could follow this road. My mind softens with the memories of last summer—all the times I drove along this road, singing loud with my roof open and my windows rolled down. I smile with these blips of the past, but my cheeks quickly weaken as I remember more. I grip the steering wheel and press down on the pedal, jolted by the acceleration. My engine's roar erases the images in my mind.

When I reach Brenton Point at the end of the drive, I slow down and pull into the lot. I park halfway along in a space away from the other cars, facing the ocean. The distant land beside me stretches out its arm but doesn't touch the open water ahead. I turn off my engine and slide my seat back to pull up my feet. I cross my legs and stare out at the horizon, breathing in the deep blue line. I sigh. Out there, the backdrop is real. The water is alive, churning out white foam and wrinkles of teal, but I'm drawn more so to the endless sky beyond. My chest rises, pulled toward the untouchable depth. Gradually, I leave my seat as my body begins to float. I smile at this secret ability of mine—this secret world I have discovered beyond the mundane responsibilities and expectations of life. When I am alone, working on this project, I feel this levitation. I wish I could exist on this plane all the time, but I am constantly being forced back down. Every time I hang out with my friends or go to work or do anything involving other people, my power slips away. Behind my eyes, a warmth pools as the strings tethered to the ground snap, and my body rises freely. I could solely live up here. I know how—I think about it all the time. As the glistening air carries me out over the waves, I look down into the darkening water to find myself sitting in the past at the bottom. I cock my head as I watch the familiar scene, remembering it all but unable to feel. Underneath the surface of the water, I am twenty-one, alone after dark on the edge of a beach. The wind must have been bitter and the sand frozen, but I didn't notice. I sat there for hours, face numb, staring out past the black waves into the void. The memory below mirrors me as I float above. Ahead of us, the alluring distance doesn't look the same, but the pull is just as strong. I look up as the cotton clouds tickle my cheeks. Sometimes I think about cutting off everyone I know—cutting out every part of my life that causes me to fall back down, but I know better. I'm not drowning like I was five years ago, but up here in the sky, I am still alone. I get the same strange sense that I'm rapidly disappearing.

I look down at my body to find myself back in my car. My chest caves as I squeeze my eyes, the pull opposite now as I collapse within, exhausted. *When will the longing stop? Will I ever be content here?* I look out again through my bug-splattered windshield across the water. I stare at the dark blue line. *Is there a way to exist in both worlds, deepened by the water yet untouchable in the sky?* When I was twenty-one, I couldn't see the line—I was positive it didn't exist—but now I'm not so sure.

A faint ding blossoms in the back of my mind. I reach for my phone, but the sound is on silent. With no new messages, the background is clear: my thirteen-year-old self glares up at me from under her baseball hat, wearing her oversized black band hoodie with her rock hands up in the air. I smile. She's the same girl from my fridge—the same girl peering back at me through my rearview mirror. I lower my baseball hat and smirk as I reenact the pose. My hands haven't forgotten. The bullhorns pop up effortlessly. Suddenly, the gravel rumbles beside me. I laugh and turn away as the car pulls up and parks, retreating inward to hide my embarrassment. As I wait for the heat in my cheeks to subside, I unlock my phone and open up the photo app to mindlessly scroll through. The blocks of color rush by like a stream, blending together in a liquid rainbow. My thumb lifts from the screen as the current stops, freezing on the images of me and my sister. I tap the blocks to look closer. We were at Governor's Ball, both smiling, dressed the same. I swipe through the memories, landing on a video of my sister. She dances in front of the stage in her long purple skirt and layers of vibrant fabrics, illuminated by the daylight and intoxicated by the sound. I was behind her, recording everything. I was watching her as she watched her favorite band.

I click off the screen, letting it go black, only to press the button again to return to the background of my younger self. In the picture, the band name printed across my hoodie is the same as the one stitched above the brim of my hat. The same band I cried for last summer when the lead singer killed himself, and no one I knew cared.

A locked-up breath breaks free between my lips as I gaze at the choppy water, waves peaking inside. The space within that pulled outward and inward before now fills with a churning energy. I open up my phone again, this time, to write a text:

> Hey, would you want to go to a rock festival with
> me this summer?

My heart pounds as my thumb hovers over "send." I reread the words quickly before releasing them into space. I sigh and look up, anxious for my sister's response.

Chapter Seventeen

I stick the bag of candy in the front pouch of my backpack and stare. I could stay home. I could rent a movie and just stay here.

Through the mesh pocket, wrapped in plastic and tied together with a bow, the candy stares back at me. I don't deserve it. The cashier didn't notice, but when she scanned the bag, I had to look away. The price didn't bother me. It wasn't even the shame. It was the promise I was making to myself—the contract I was secretly signing as I scribbled my signature on the bottom of the receipt. I can't eat this candy, not yet. Not until I ride my bike to the beach and watch the outdoor movie on my blanket alone.

I take a deep breath and swing the backpack over my shoulders. The weightlessness surprises me. I'm used to the rocks. I head into the basement to grab my bike and push it out the back door, bursting free into the cool night air. I smile, absorbing the breeze. Suddenly, I'm not afraid. I lift my leg over the seat and begin to pedal, invigorated by the blur of passing trees. I am young and rebellious again, escaping from my childhood home. The hood on my sweatshirt hugs my neck, protecting me the way it did when I was thirteen. I ride fast down the street—a phantom in the dark racing toward the edge of the hill. Gravity takes over as the twinkling lights across the reservoir come into view. They melt into the water, reaching toward me, drawing me down. I squeeze the brake, turning right at the stop sign, and follow the winding road toward the beach. Over the crash of the waves and roar of the wind, I can hear the people. The temperature drops. The monstrous blow-up screen on the beach sways, beckoning me close as I drift toward the parking lot. My wheels roll slow.

Aware of the young man standing near the bike rack, I avert my eyes. He watches me through the dark as I get off my bike.

"I'll take that."

His hand reaches out for the handlebar, but I quickly pull it away.

"I can do it." I walk my bike to the other side of the rack, pushing the front wheel into the first open slot. He hovers behind as I uncoil the lock from the seat post. I turn toward him.

"Thank you, but I really don't need your help."

He ignores me and moves closer.

"It's my job." He puts his hand on the seat. The lock shakes in my hand as I struggle to feed the cable through the rack.

"Okay, but seriously, I've got it."

He removes his hand from the seat and retreats a few steps back. I strain the ends of the lock together, pulling them close, but not close enough. I dab the sweat from my upper lip with the back of my hand and untwist the cable to try again. The cotton interior of my sweatshirt clings. I roll up my sleeves the way I used to in eighth grade when I had nothing but a tank top underneath. Hunching, I click the ends together, jumbling up the letters with my thumbs. My body is tight and small—a familiar suffocation trapped in the confines of my sweatshirt. I can feel the relentless eyes behind me. I spin the letters around once more. I can't tell if I'm being paranoid.

"Thanks." I peek up at the man still lingering and then walk away. I grip the straps of my backpack and pull the bag close as I move toward the opening in the stone wall. Down the steps and around the towering screen, the crowd takes over. Three hundred voices hit me at once, crawling and morphing together into one infested sound. I walk along the perimeter, stopping short as two manic kids run by. They disappear into the night as I continue on to the very back, furthest from the screen and closest to the water. I unzip my backpack and lay out the blanket, ignoring the bunched up corners as I sit down. The wet sand immediately soaks through.

I roll onto my shins, but the cold dampness spots my knees. I pull the blanket up toward the crowd, straining my neck around the two people ahead to search for a better spot, but everyone has a chair.

I sigh, settling on the crack of screen. The two chatty friends in front of me lean in, sealing up my already obstructed view, but it doesn't matter. My butt is wet, and the sweat from before has dried cold. A shiver runs up my spine. I gather the sandy corners of my blanket and pull them close, leaning my floppy backpack up against my side. The plastic bag in the mesh crackles. My body is planted now, unable to move, but the saturation continues to expand. I don't know how I'm going to make it through this movie.

The screen glows blue over the crowd. I scan the alien world, head low, searching for anyone I recognize. A familiar laugh jolts me. Cautiously, I turn to the sound, eyes freezing on the unmistakable figure. A few yards away in the midst of the silhouettes, Steve stands. He laughs again, the uninhibited waves disturbing as they surge through me. I crumble low, but still, I can't hide from the scene. I watch as he smiles, lit up by the screen but more so from the girl standing beside him. I don't know her. I've never seen her before, but that doesn't snuff the licks of fire catching in my chest. I look down at my lap—my damp, dirty, blanketed nest. I am alone. I am not independent or brave or admirable. I am pathetic and sad. Hot tears form. Behind me, a couple settles in, unfolding their chairs. I suck back the tears, absorbing them down. I lift up my chin.

Steve is still standing, but the girl has disappeared. He looks around, eyebrows flat and serious as his gaze drifts closer to the back of the crowd. Our eyes meet. He smiles and waves, but I don't move. I wait just to be sure, but he continues to look right at me. I muster a smile and wave back, phony confidence extended high in the air. His eyes squint, and his smile fades. The air grows heavy as both our arms sink back down.

"There you are!"

I turn around. Two girls rush past me, heading directly to Steve. His attention shifts as they crash into him. He laughs, arms wide. My cheeks flood with heat as I look down. He wasn't waving at me. Behind my rib cage, a space opens, pulling me in. I want to disappear. Underneath the dirty blanket, on the inside of my crossed thigh, there is a hole in my leggings. I crawl inside, hiding within the torn fabric. The couple behind me whispers. My ears hear everything—they've always been too sharp. I listen to the murmurs as my shoulders hunch and the back of my neck burns. They're talking about me. I can feel it. If I were them, I'd probably be talking about me too. I clench my jaw, squeezing the cavity in my ears and closing my eyes. This isn't paranoia—I know the difference. The couple saw everything, and now they're laughing at my shame.

The sand goes black for a moment. I look up. The speakers crackle to life as the movie begins. I don't see Steve. Everyone has settled now, blended together, yet somehow, I am separate, drifting further and further away. I stare at the sliver of screen, picking up colors and faces, but not making sense of anything. The sound from the speakers blows away, down the beach, too weak to cut through the steady breeze. I shiver. The bag of candy crinkles under my arm. There are a dozen reasons to leave and only one pathetic reason to stay. I peel off the blanket. I don't care about my pact anymore. I just want to go home.

Staying low to the ground, I stuff the blanket into my backpack, wet sand and all. I zipper it fast and grab the straps to slip away, but the couple behind me sees.

"Where are you going?" the girl asks. They both stare with open eyes. Their curiosity is sincere.

"I can't see or hear anything. I'm going home."

"No, don't." The boy reaches out. "You should stay."

The warmth from his words shocks me. My body stiffens. They did see. They did talk about what happened. I turn away, moving fast across the sand.

As I climb up the steps to the parking lot, I breathe in. The man by the bikes hasn't left. I approach too quickly, flashing a smile as I bend down to untangle the lock. My knees shake.

"Leaving already?"

His question slithers in the air. I keep my eyes down. I pull my bike free from the rack and hop on, escaping into the dark. I pedal fast, the wind pushing against me as I move toward the hill. I don't bother shifting. I stand up, pushing down hard on the pedals, determined to get home.

I peel out on my gravel driveway as I squeeze the break. I pull out my key and open the basement door. My handlebars catch on the railing of the stairs. I twist and pull until the bike bursts loose, crashing down. The metal scrapes my calf, but I don't feel the sting. I let the wheel bang down the last step, ignoring the chain's unhinged rattle. In the back corner, I discard the bike and watch it collapse—broken kickstand in the air, spokes spinning. I turn away and head upstairs.

In the kitchen, I untangle myself from the backpack, remembering the disgusting blanket inside. I grab the straps and carry the bag to the back room, dumping the soiled contents into my hamper. Grains of sand scatter the floor. My cat meows. I storm past her as I begin to pace back and forth between my living room and kitchen. I drag my nails up the side of my neck, the tension still building in my jaw. I move to the bathroom.

I tear open the shower curtain and turn on the water, the rush screaming up the pipes. I pull my hand away as the cold rain pours down. I turn around. The mirror stops me. Between the two bright lights on the wall, my reflection stares back unnervingly clear. My hair is frizzy, my cheeks puffy and splotched with red. I can't lean in, but I can't look away. All I can do is watch as my eyes scan down, falling to the words written so boldly across my chest: *Wolf Hollow.* The camping trip Steve and I took together. His faded smile flashes again. I see myself through his eyes, sitting small in the dark, pitiful and alone, clinging to the memory stamped black on my sweatshirt. The heat swells. I look like a fool. I rip off the sweatshirt, my tattered leggings, and my underwear too. I chuck it all into the hamper and dig out my candy from the backpack on the floor. I tear off the bow, sticking my hand in the bag to shovel up a mouthful of gummy sugar. I pace as I eat, moving into the hallway, the kitchen, the living room, cycling back to start again. My cat meows from the couch this time. I look down. She's sitting up straight, eyes wide, ears alert. Just above her and across the room, another mirror stares back at me. I swallow the sticky lump in my throat, stunned by my empty expression. I am exposed, naked with my fingers deep in the plastic, mindlessly searching for my next consumable fix. I look away. The tears form, but they're not hot like before. I stare at the bag clenched in my hands, nearly empty with nothing but white granulated sand at the bottom. The last pieces of candy lie stranded on the beach.

I walk back to the kitchen and throw the crumbled up remains away. Grabbing the rose quartz from my bookshelf, I follow the sound of falling water. I switch the flow from above to a bath, stepping into the tub as the warm water pools. I sit down. The wavy wet line tickles up my skin as I cup the rose quartz and press its imperfect pink body to my chest. I hold it in place. When the water is high enough, I close my eyes and slip beneath the surface. The tension in my jaw floats away as I let go of my breath and allow myself to sink down into the blush-toned womb.

Chapter Eighteen

"Melissa?"

I look up and grab my purse. I follow my psychiatrist down the hall into her office. She sits at her desk as I sink down beside her into the usual metal chair, my face squeezing into a smile. She doesn't notice. She adjusts her glasses and opens my file.

"Okay, so last time I saw you, you were sleeping too much and still having problems with drinking."

My smile drops to the floor. She glances over.

"How are you feeling now?"

"Right now?" I laugh. She lifts her chin and squints. "For the most part, I've actually been feeling pretty good."

"And how's your drinking been?"

"Fine. I haven't really been drinking at all." She leans back and crosses her arms. The space between us is cold and empty. I sit frozen, feet planted still but shivering underneath her hard stare. "I don't go out anymore. I'm trying to be more independent and do stuff on my own."

"Are you isolating?"

The question slaps like a wet fish across my face.

"What? No." I laugh, trying to wipe away the residual slime, but her mouth holds firm. My skin grows scales. "I'm not isolating. The only thing my friends care about is drinking and meeting boys. I'm trying to be healthy and stay away from all that shit."

She doesn't flinch. "And how's that going?"

"Good! No more blacking out or eating the entire McDonald's menu at 2:00 a.m."

She nods her head and leans forward over my chart. "Is that the only time you binge eat?"

My lips seal. She uncaps a pen, eyes glued, ready on the page. I swallow, adjusting the elastic band around my waist.

"No, but drinking makes it worse."

She takes off her glasses and breathes in. My legs cross as she swivels to face me again. I wish it was winter. I wish I was wearing more clothes.

"Drinking makes everything worse." She sighs. "I'm glad you're staying away from alcohol, but you can't avoid your friends. You need to find other ways to hang out with them."

"I know…" I look down. On the edge of my nail, where the sliver of skin separates, I pick and pull. There are two ways to view me—two extreme and opposing views. I rip off the hangnail, thinking about last night—thinking about Steve's face and my own disgusted reflection in the mirror. I press the puffed skin around my nail, snuffing out the pain, trying to hold on to the other side. "I really am doing well, though. Most days, I feel empowered being alone."

"But you're still binge eating?"

Another slap to the face. I bite my nail, gnawing on her words, trying to spit out a response. "I was actually proud last night. I didn't—"

"Let me check something."

Her chair squeaks as she rolls across the floor. She grabs her phone from the desk. "I wonder if other people have experienced binge eating as a side effect from Latuda."

As she thumbs up the screen, I look around. The search is pointless. Still, I wait patiently, letting us both believe there's an easy fix.

"Hmm, not too common, but a few people have reported eating issues too."

I watch her face as it continues to glow dumbly in the screen. I look to the wall, to the gold-brushed frames hung evenly over her desk. I can't read the dates. There's a glare on the glass.

"We could ween you off Latuda and try a different pill…"

"No."

Her eyes flash up. My chest trembles, remembering the slew of pills, the restless nights, the tremors, and my wounded face. I cave in to the right, hiding the dark patch—the self-inflicted scar—against my shoulder. Tucked in that space, I find my dad. I find his averted, yet constantly aware eyes. "Honestly, the eating thing is nothing new. I've been dealing with it for years, but I can handle it. I stopped myself last night."

"Really?" She puts her phone back on the desk, facedown. "What did you do to stop yourself?"

My mouth opens, but the words hesitate at the ledge. They're too fragile. The blocks of bright light above will shatter them on impact. I swallow the most vulnerable pieces—the details only my counselor would understand.

"I took a bath instead."

Her brows scrunch. "And that helped?"

"Yeah." I breathe in. "I actually felt pretty great after."

She frowns. "Hm." She slips her glasses back on and scans fast to the bottom of my chart. She closes the manila folder and gets up to grab my pills. I take the handful of samples as she returns to her desk to sign the checkout sheet.

"All right, so I won't see you for another month." She caps the pen and hands me the double-layered sheet. I grab the paper, but she holds on, looking me in the eye. "You need friends."

I nod fast, and she lets go. My ears ring as I move down the hall and wait for the receptionist to peel off the top sheet. She says something as she slides back the pale pink page, but I can't hear. I stuff the copy in my purse and leave. The ringing gives way to buried thoughts as I drive.

By the time I reach the bridge, the sun is almost down. I should go home. I should be safe and give myself a break, but beyond the Newport ramp, I keep going. I drive to Portsmouth, to my usual hiking spot, and park to strap on the familiar weight. I plug in my headphones to blast the music—to blast away the fear as I enter the dark woods, as I did in eighth grade—but underneath the blaring riffs and the throat-tearing screams, I can still hear the mental sound.

You're fat.
You're ugly.
You're a slut with no friends.

Chapter Nineteen

My mom is chatty as usual, but I don't mind. I crave her company today. As she talks, I peer up into the rearview to check on the two dogs nestled in my back seat. They're so quiet, it's easy to forget they're there.

"So your dad is doing well—busy at work but good—and I saw my parents the other day. They're doing well too."

I smile. My mom's conversation routines are comforting today. I drive slowly down the hill toward the beach, the sun high and hazy in the sky. Through the crack in my window, the warm breeze tickles my skin, mellow fluff in the air. My mom turns to me.

"How many walks do we have left?"

"This is actually the last one, and all I have to do is let the dogs play in the yard."

"Wow, easy day."

Skipping my usual turn, I drive on toward the street that runs along the reservoir. I choose this alternate route with my mom in mind, but as I wait for a break in the traffic, I wonder why I don't always go this way. The reservoir sparkles in the distance like a pool of liquid diamonds. The dancing light catches her attention as she stares off at the glistening mounds. We both breathe in deep, a moment of silence. She and I are having a good day.

Across traffic on the other side, the reservoir only appears in blips between the trees and tall houses. My mom resumes talking. I go back to listening, eyes focused on the road ahead.

Suddenly, my body freezes. I see the black truck. It sits in the driveway on the left up ahead, dauntingly real. My mom's voice fades as a heavy silence takes over. There is a resistance in the air. The wind pushes me backward, deep into my seat, but my foot on the pedal remains stiff, locked into place. I continue forward. As I get closer, I don't want to look, but of course, I do. I'm compelled every time. Beyond the black truck, up the driveway and up the ladder leaning on the side of the house, my breath stops. I never expected to see him again. Quickly, I turn back to the road and drive on, a cold chasm in my chest expanding.

I can't turn my head, but out of the corner of my eye, my mom's lips move. There is no sound. The bubble around me is thick and impenetrable. Words and wind evaporate at its touch. I continue driving, taking turns automatically, thoughtless inside my vacuum-sealed world. I have been here before.

The images through my windshield morph into white plaster—my cracked wall by the front door. I'm standing there again, stuck and helpless, the way I was at the end of last summer. There is no sound, no time, no reality in that wall. Just blankness and hairline fractures. Hours passed. I only knew because the clock behind me kept skipping ahead.

The road filters back as I reach the driveway of my last stop. I park and turn off the ignition, turning slowly to my mom, but she doesn't seem to have noticed any change. Trails of ghost arms follow her animated hands. Her voice is muffled—underwater nonsense in my ears. I blink hard, trying to burst the bubble and reset the glitches in my brain. Eventually, the phantom images catch up with reality, and the volume returns to normal. She says something about lasagna—a new sauce recipe. I stare blankly, wanting to understand, but her words hit my hollow cheeks and fall flat on the floor.

"Should we head in?"

This, I hear.

"Yeah, um, I'll meet you in the back."

I walk around my car to lead my mom to the side gate. Just before closing her door, I see the dogs in the back seat. I shake my head and scoop them up to carry them to the backyard. I need to get my head on straight.

In the house, the three dogs waiting for me spin around and bark in the kitchen. I step over the gate and unlock the slider, watching them scurry down the backsteps. I can hear my mom's voice outside as she greets them. I move to the sink to refill the water bowls, carefully placing them back on the mat and then returning to the faucet to let the water run ice cold over my hands.

In the backyard, I find my mom by the side of the house, sitting on an Adirondack chair. The liveliest of the five dogs is prancing around her, nuzzling his head under her arm, trying to get her to play. She laughs and looks at me.

"This guy is hilarious! So full of energy."

I try to smile, but the corners of my mouth are heavy. I look around the yard, silently counting the four other dogs, and then I move to the chair beside her.

"So your father and I have started watching a pretty good show. It's about a woman who…"

My mom's voice trails off again. I look to the far end of the property, past the fence and beyond the overgrown weeds and brambles. The reservoir twinkles, a million desperate messages in Morse code. As I stare, the reflections blur and blend into one. The wavering light fills my mind. Everything around it fades to black until there is nothing left except my painful memories and that evasive white light.

"The main character though is so intriguing. And the relationship between her and the other…"

I listen for a pause, but it never comes. Unlocking my gaze, I turn back toward my mom, waiting for the puffs of blindness to fade away. She keeps talking. I want to be patient. I nod slowly and breathe in. There's a pressure in my ears, a building tension in my jaw. I can't wait any longer. Under her constant stream of words, I speak low in tone, "*I just saw Tim.*"

"What? When?"

I turn to look at her. Bulbs of light flash where her face should be.

"Just now, on our way over here."

"Why didn't you say something?"

I don't answer. Her face comes into view as the illusions disappear. She's on the edge of her seat, eyes wide, hand gripped on the armrest of her chair. I lean back. Her lips are too tight—too certain and extreme. I can't tell her how I feel. I can't even begin to explain. I'd have to go back to the beginning to show her the other side, but would she be convinced? *How can I tell a story that's already been tainted by the ending? How can I express my feelings when I can't feel the majority of them without covering my mouth in shame?*

"Where was he? What was he doing? Did he see you?"

Her questions are sharp. They feel like accusations.

"He didn't see me. I wasn't trying to be seen." I drag my nails up my scalp and clench a fistful of my hair. "You don't know what the fuck happened. No one does. You only came at the end."

I look down, nails pressed into my brow with my palms, hiding my face. I keep my jaw locked as a guttural scream tears up my throat. Every muscle in my body tightens.

"I stopped eating and sleeping for fuck's sake. Why can't you understand that? I stopped eating and sleeping for *five fucking days!*"

I stand up from my chair to pace around. My hands are shaking.

"Honey, I know. I didn't say—"

"*Anyone* would have lost it. After five days, the same shit would have happened to anyone."

I stop to stare at her. My gaze is cold. The anger radiates through every layer of my being—a familiar possession. I can't stay this way though as I take her in. She's small and fragile, afraid like she was last summer. I turn away, clawing at the monster inside my head—the one that she so clearly sees.

We both fall silent. The pain inside me peaks and then coils back up from where it came. My voice is small.

"Sometimes I think about getting off my pills."

The surge comes from my mom this time.

"Absolutely not! How could you even think that? After all you went through? After everything…"

Her voice trails off, words shaky. I watch her brows scrunch up as she starts to crumble. I can't do this to her again.

"You're right, Mom. I'm sorry. It was a stupid thing to say. I didn't mean it."

I turn away from her trembling lips to walk around the yard. Three of the dogs are sitting by the sliding door, waiting to go back in. The other two are sniffing around the far edge of the fence, poking their tiny heads between the spaces.

You were hospitalized before. Chances are, without medication, you'll end up here again.

The nurse's words run cold again over my skin. I rub my arm and look back at my mom. She's watching me, her eyes plead.

"I won't get off my pills, Mom. I promise."

She breathes, believing this time I'm telling the truth. Eleven months have passed since that nurse pulled me aside, but her words are still real. The fear trumps everything.

Chapter Twenty

While pulling my backpack of rocks out from the back seat, a chocolate lab approaches. I kneel down.

"Hello, sweet puppy. How are you?"

Her muzzle is speckled white and her eyes clouded, but still, she stares, tail wagging.

"Maggie!" An old man walks around the backside of my car. "Magg—oh, there you are. Sorry, I didn't realize anyone was over here. We just got back from our hike."

I wave my hand as he pulls out a leash and clips it to her collar. "Don't worry about it. I'm a dog walker. I don't mind at all."

"You're a dog walker? Do you do pet sitting too?"

I nibble at the flesh on the inside of my cheek. "I do," I say slowly. The old man's eyes light up. I know I shouldn't, but I reach in my purse and grab him a card. "My schedule is pretty full, but I'll do my best."

He smiles as I hand him the card, and then he reaches into his pocket. He pulls out his wallet and begins to dig through the tightly packed sleeves.

"Hold on, I have a business card too somewhere in here." Maggie sits patiently beside him, looking at me with her misty gaze. I cock my head, and her tail thumps the ground. "Here it is!"

The old man wiggles the card free and hands it to me. In the middle, printed large and navy blue, a strange word stares at me. My eyebrows furrow as I search for his name and address. The expected information is there, but it's scattered small around the perimeter, centered around and emphasizing the peculiar word: *Lorelei*. The back is blank. I flip it over and look up, surprised to find that Maggie and the old man have disappeared. Through my car window, I can see them settling into the truck parked beside me. The door slams shut, and the engine rumbles. I watch as they pull away, waving with the card still in my hand. Alone in the parking lot, I read the word once more and then toss the card on my passenger seat. I strap on my backpack, lock my car, and head out, moving steadily into the trees.

When I reach the map in the center of the woods, I realize I forgot my phone. My headphones lie useless, zippered inside my waist-strap pocket. I pull them out and untangle the chord, glancing back down the dirt trail. I've only walked five minutes, but still, I sigh. I bunch the chord back up in my pocket and continue on, breathing in the muggy air.

As I step out from the trees and walk along the vast, clear-cut field, my ears expand. The cars glide by in the distance—alien wind from a faraway world. All around, the heat buzzes, stinging my cheeks and bleaching the grass. My eyes tear. I squint and look down, rocks pounding with each step. Trying to focus on my next burden, I close my eyes, but without my music, the rocks all seem to blend together. They clop against my back—one giant, inseparable mass.

I groan and lift the backpack higher, turning right into the next patch of trees. The shade slows my pace and vacuums out all sound. With my hands gripped around my shoulder straps and my elbows tucked close to my sides, I peer around. I was here just yesterday, but somehow the woods have changed. The wall of trunks closes in on me like a tapering tunnel, their dense arms sealing out the air. I keep my eyes ahead as I will my legs to move. My thighs are thick and my feet heavy, but I can't give in. Despite the dread, something is luring me on.

When I reach the soccer field, I hug the perimeter with my head down as always, ignoring the laughter sprinting across the grass. I follow the path along the chain-link fence, peeking up as I turn the corner to spy on the children. The warmth from my cheeks drains as a cold ripple stiffens my spine. There are no children. The field is empty. The wind blows, disturbing the hairs on the back of my neck and trembling through the goal post's netting. My eyes soften as I stare, watching the invisible laughter float across the field and materialize in the past. I am small. The woods stand behind me as my classmates run around, distracted by the kickball high in the air. For a moment, I am free—released from their hateful eyes. The trees behind me beckon, whispering escape. I step backward, pulled by an increasing force. I turn around and bolt, immediately smacked in the face by sharp leaves. The woods have vanished. In front of me, a wall of Rhododendrons laughs. I turn around as I feel for the bag of rocks on my back. It's still there, and the soccer field is still vacant. I continue along the path, moving fast as I disappear into the brush.

I charge ahead, fingers white gripped around my straps. The path curves as the bushes to my right fade away. I look to the yellow meadow, searching for comfort in its grassy waves, but the dead stalks stand frozen. My feet stop as I stare at the painting. I am paralyzed, stuck in my body. The still life draws me in as the memories crawl up from the ground. I watch in horror as the bony fingers pop up through the dirt, resurrected scenes from last summer. I am helpless, eyes wide, as my mind unburies the pieces.

"Melissa, stop! Please stop! I don't want to, but I'm going to have to block you."

I was shaking, the phone in my hand. The dogs were in the yard, off in the distance when the simultaneous texts started rolling in. *Allie and Tim.* They were saying the same thing. With the phone to my ear, I could hear the laughter, condescending and cruel as I stood terrified.

"Melissa, what are you talking about? I'm not with Allie. I'm at work right now."

My voice was low and heavy. I was speaking from somewhere deep within.

"I swear. I'm not sleeping with her!"

"*Slept.* Not sleeping. *Slept.*"

The phone went silent—thick and hot. The seconds burned painfully slow. His nerves slithered through the receiver—a different laugh this time. I could tell he was lying. I could tell because I used to laugh like that too. He went cold. His voice turned small.

"You already know."

I shake my head, but the memories keep digging up. I see myself crying in the car, driving to my next dog stop, begging for the truth.

"Just tell me! Just say it!"

"Melissa, you know. You already know."

The meadow returns, towering above me. I'm on the ground with my backpack still strapped, hands clasped around my skull. My mind is swollen, pressure fracturing the bone. I try to contain the headache, but it builds, pumping anxiety through my veins. I hear Allie's voice this time. Her words were small—emotionless.

"He didn't look at all like the pictures you showed me. I didn't know he drove a red truck."

I groan. The e-mails stream. I didn't remember before, but now all my hateful words return. I close my eyes and hide my face as the pages scroll up the glowing screen. I was typing fast. I couldn't stop writing. I couldn't stop hitting send. All I wanted was a straight answer, but by the fourth sleepless night, I had lost all control.

I bury my head—my arms wrapped tightly around my knees. The backpack strains my shoulders, tugging me open, but I hold on tight. I have to. I can't bear exposing myself to the destruction I've caused, but even more so, I can't stand the notion of never knowing the truth. I'm stuck, caught in the subtleties and the web of infinite stories. *What was real and what was only in my mind?* I lift my head and stare at the dirt path, longing for the distance around the next curve. My body is still frozen—hand tapping the kitchen faucet hour after hour, mindlessly, like I was at the end of last summer. I was stuck then, and I am still stuck now. Nothing has changed. *Was I the girl driven mad by love or the girl driven mad by circumstance? How can I move on if I don't know what to blame? How can I move on if I don't know where I need to heal?*

The wind blows. My gaze shifts toward the golden weeds. A wave rolls through the meadow, breathing life into the scene as my lungs fill with air. In the center of the yellow grass, I see a girl—she is the thirteen-year-old me. She kicks the dirt and screams, distant in time and within a different meadow but existing just the same. She nods her head to the music blasting in her ears. Her school backpack lies discarded on the ground. I watch her thrash and punch the air, her fiery energy charging through my veins. I grip my straps and push myself up, lowering my head as I begin to move, glaring up through my brows. With each step, I feel stronger. My feet pound against the packed dirt, my rocks solid like armor on my back. The little girl screams, and I scream too, belting out the lyrics to our favorite rock song. I forgot how much I love anger. I forgot how much I depend on it to power me through.

As I march on, I smile, remembering something my dad once said: *Anger plus good direction equals passion.*

My chin rises as I repeat the words and reenter the trees. The tunnel expands this time, making room for me.

Chapter Twenty-One

I climb up the bed of rock on the far edge of Pebble Beach and turn back toward the path. I'm early. My hand gravitates to the phone in my purse, but I reach for the yellow tapestry under my arm instead. I lay it over the top of the rock as the wind blows gently, smoothing out the wrinkles and folds. With no one around, I settle onto the vibrant patch of fabric, crossing my legs and scooting forward to find a comfortable spot. The rock is warm. The waves roll, peaceful underneath the sleepy sun. I smile and breathe in. My hand drifts mindlessly toward my purse again, but I leave the bag zipped and rest my hand on top. I'd rather not know when Laura's coming. I'd rather she simply arrive.

The pebbles crunch behind me. I turn around to find Laura dressed in a flowy long skirt and a floppy gray sweatshirt. She moves like the grass in the distance, blowing closer, tall and graceful with her long dark hair. She smiles. I light up. I haven't seen her in months. I gather my purse and tapestry to meet her halfway along the beach. Up close, she looks the same, but her gentle eyes always surprise me. They soften as she opens her arms and wraps me in, holding me like she always does, much longer than most. I don't try to break free. The pebbles click and tap as they tumble in the waves—a soothing symphony.

She breathes in and sighs. "Hello, friend."

Our arms fall away as we each step back. I pull out the tapestry and let it float to the ground, crumbling on top as she melts beside me.

"How are you?" she asks. Her gaze is soft but delves too deep. My words burst out fast.

"Good. How are you?"

She doesn't seem to mind the hardness in my voice. She turns to the ocean and inhales slow, her chin sinking slightly as she releases her breath.

"A lot just happened. I don't even know where to begin."

Her eyes rest ahead, somewhere across the water. I skim the wavy surface and then look back at her, waiting for her to speak.

"Thank you for meeting up with me by the way. I know this was last minute."

"Of course!" I nod quickly. "You can always depend on me."

She glances over and smiles. As she returns to the distance ahead, I press my thumb against my lips and look down, remembering her text. Initially, I didn't want to respond. I put away my phone and ignored the message, focusing instead on my busy schedule. I couldn't imagine meeting up with a friend. The idea seemed stressful, but now that I'm here, I don't know what I was dreading. I scratch my bottom lip as she sighs. Her hair swirls in the wind.

"You're the best. You have no idea how much that means to me. I don't usually open up to people when I'm going through stuff. This is all new to me."

"Same!" I shout, hands flying open. I reel my arms back in and lower my voice. "I have the same problem. I've always depended on boyfriends for support, but I never felt comfortable reaching out to friends."

Her energy shoots out this time.

"Exactly!" The brilliance in her eyes peaks too fast, fading just as quickly as she turns away again. I lean in toward her. The words in my mouth dissolve as she takes in a slow breath. I feel funny staring at her profile. Running my hands over my stubbly knees, I search for something to pick. A small scab flakes easily.

"That's actually why I'm here. Max and I broke up."

I widen my eyes and open my mouth. I knew this was coming. All day, I had a feeling he was the reason she wanted to meet me here.

"I'm so sorry. What happened?"

She breathes in through her flared nose and releases a heavy sigh. "So much happened, and it all *just* happened. He ruined my birthday!" She closes her eyes and runs her fingers across her scalp. I can feel the tingles along my head. I scratch, digging up grains of dead skin. My hand drops back down as she opens her eyes and looks at me. "He changed so much. In the end, he didn't even seem to care."

A puff of sand sprays our backs as a dog tramples between us. He wiggles in front of Laura, long fluffy tail whacking me in the arm as he licks her chin. She laughs.

"Well, hello there! Where did you come from?"

I stare blankly as Laura's head rolls back, cheeks rounded and bright, kiss spots glistening in the sun. I reach out to pet the dog, trying to smile. I wish I could feel emotions the way Laura feels her own—so spontaneously without judgment or thought. I'm still stuck in the moment before. I'm still trying to figure out how to react to a broken heart.

"Charley! Come here, Charley! Leave those girls alone."

The dog rushes off to join a middle-aged couple by the path. I turn back to Laura, who's smiling and waving at the owners.

"Dogs are so funny. They can tell when someone needs love."

My back straightens. I never knew she thought about animals that way. I assumed I was the only one. She looks to the water again. I follow her gaze. The waves curl and snake through the pebbles' cracks, touching the tapestry's hemmed edge and Laura's bare feet. The yellow threads darken under her toes.

"You know, I almost brought my bathing suit. Water is so healing."

I smile, remembering something Shamus told me when I was young.

"My high school boyfriend believed the same thing. He used to tell me to take a shower whenever I felt like crap." I shake my head, smirking. "Or maybe that was just his polite way of telling me I smelled."

We both laugh, turning to each other. Her cheeks are pillows as I rest in her eyes.

"We are so similar. We've been through so much of the same thing." She sighs, allowing her smile to flow with the wind out to sea. She stares at the horizon. "Even though what I'm going through right now hurts, I feel comforted knowing that I've been in love before. I loved Max, but nothing compares to the love I had with Chris in high school."

I look down at my lap. My hands squeeze each other as the words crumble out. "I don't even know what love is anymore."

"Yeah, me neither."

My head lifts, chin raised by her clear voice. We keep our attention aligned, slightly below the sinking sun.

"Thank god, I have you," she says. "The old me would be curled up in a ball alone at home right now."

I nod my head. "Yep. I know *exactly* what you mean."

Absorbing the blue, salted breeze, we sit silently along the shore. The clicking pebbles tickle my ears as my hands slowly unclench. They lie still, resting together, underneath the hazy sky.

"Okay, I think I'm ready to talk about what happened."

I turn toward her, chest open and relaxed.

"Go ahead. I'm listening."

Chapter Twenty-Two

The greyhound stops and pulls back at the corner of Touro Park. She bows her head and resists the leash as I try to move forward.

"What's up, Athena?"

I loosen the choke collar around her neck, slipping my fingers underneath to rub her soft skin. The fur fades along the edges of her throat. I follow her pointed nose, turned to the sidewalk across from the park. She stares at a white plastic sign a few yards ahead.

I hold the leash down by my side as we move closer to read the words. A blue arrow at the bottom points right to a glass door tucked between two large windows. I've never noticed this store before. I crack open the door, peeking in with Athena beside me. On the far side, a woman behind the counter smiles.

"Come in! We don't mind dogs."

We walk in, moving unnaturally slow along the pristine tile. From floor to ceiling, everything is white or encased in glass. The cool-conditioned air hits my skin. I step lightly toward the counter as Athena's nails tap across the floor. As we reach the other side, the woman leans in, her bracelets jingling beneath her long satin sleeves. I pull down the end of my bunched-up gym shorts, embarrassed by my exposed skin.

"Were you looking for something in particular?"

"Yeah, actually I am. I saw your sign about crystal-infused water out front."

She perks up. "Oh yes, right over here!"

She walks around the counter and leads me to the tall glass case by the window. She points at the strange cylinder sculptures displayed on the middle shelf. Inside each, a colored crystal sits in a transparent chamber, surrounded by water.

"These are our special crystal-infused water bottles. They each come with a crystal already inside, but you can swap them out for whatever crystal you prefer. It's best if you allow time for the new vibrations to infuse the water though. We recommend waiting at least an hour."

I lean in toward the glass, staring at the bottle closest to me. The lavender rock glistens—its beauty multiplied by the refracted sunlight shining through. I try to imagine the bottle outside the case, surrounded by dog hair in my sticky cup holder. Athena stands quietly beside me, eyes half closed. She yawns.

"How much are they?"

"A hundred and twenty."

I tighten my grip on the leash and back away.

"Would you like me to take one out for you?"

"No, that's okay." I turn around. "I think I just want to browse."

"By all means! Take your time."

As she returns to the counter, the thought to sneak out crosses my mind, but I'm drawn to a small table case instead on the opposite side of the store. I look down through the glass at a smoky, sea foam stone. Its heart-shaped body is small and smooth. I'm afraid to ask the price.

"Oh, that's on sale! All of the heart-shaped stones are fifteen dollars."

My eyes widen. "Can I see this one?"

"Of course!" She comes over to unlock the side of the case and reaches in. Up close, I can see the veins of dark blue and deepening pools of fluorescent green. The stone is cool in my hands. I cradle it in my palm, resisting the urge to press it to my cheek and warm it against my skin.

"What's it called?"

"Labradorite. Have you heard of it?"

I shake my head.

"Oh well, today's your lucky day! Labradorite is an incredible stone. It's supposed to bring magic into your life."

I keep my eyes on the stone as she talks, tilting it inside my cupped hands. The color melts over the rounded edges, alive and fluid like the mysterious changing hues of an iris. Her words are far-fetched, but not entirely unbelievable.

"Okay, I'll take it."

I wait patiently as she rings me out and wraps up my purchase with tissue paper, tucked inside a small teal bag. She pulls out a white lace ribbon and ties the bag's handles together, smiling as she hands me the receipt.

"Enjoy."

I take the bag and head outside, immediately stopping around the corner to fish out the stone. I tear off the tissue and toss it in the nearby trash along with the crumbled-up bag, raising the stone up between my fingers. Flecks of light shimmer in the sun. A car roars by, blowing my hair in my face as I squeeze my hand closed around the tiny heart. With no one behind me, I open the collar of my shirt and stuff the stone inside the top of my bra. I walk Athena back home and continue my day, patting the left side of my chest every now and then to make sure the small lump is still there.

Back home, I drop my purse to the floor and sigh. I pull out the stone, warm from my breast, and place it on the coffee table as I move to the bathroom to peel off my clothes and turn on the shower. The sweat and grime washes away down the drain, but the water can't rinse out the disappointment on my face. All day, I was wait-ing—waiting and hoping and looking for magic even though I knew I was being ridiculous. I step out of the tub and dry off, putting on my same pajamas to head into the kitchen to make my same salad and watch the same show as I do every night. Sitting on the floor of my living room, I poke at the chicken with my fork, watching the wet pieces wiggle across the lettuce. The edges along the slice are smooth, rubberlike in their processed perfection. I stab the meat and chew, but the taste isn't the same. I look to the TV, avoiding the heart-shaped rock on the table as I force down the rest of my meal. In the kitchen, I clean off my plate and stick it in the dishwasher, lingering near my open cabinet. I'm turned off by everything but still hungry for more. I groan and rub my face. I push at my brow and lean against my hand as the cravings start to swirl. I look to my phone. It beckons me from the other room. I think about all the restaurants I could dial—the gooey salty cheese and greasy red meat between my teeth. I close my eyes. The temptation is too easy. I wouldn't even have to step outside or change my clothes. I could satisfy the craving with one quick ring. I dig my knuckles into my temple and move to the window. I crack open the blind and look up to the sky. There is no moon, no stars—only black space between my neighbors' rooftops.

I breathe deep through my nose and exhale the same. The blind snaps shut as I drop my hand and back away. I'm surrounded by white walls. Every corner in my apartment is another dead end— another dead space for my body to curl up in and waste away. I haven't escaped the hospital's eighth floor. I'm still trapped inside the locked, solitary room.

I change fast, grabbing my purse to head out the door. I start up my car and begin to drive, pulled along by the dark space above me with no destination in mind. I pass first beach, leaning over my steering wheel to search the open sky. Through the strip of city lights, I continue up the hill and down to second beach, where a strange orange mound grows in the distance. Eyes wide, I realize I'm looking at the moon. I float toward the alien sun—the pavement like a river guiding me to the eastern-most edge of the beach. I park and step out, mouth open as the enormous moon pulls me across the sand. Free from the treetops and the curves of the land, the tangerine ball sits full and heavy on the horizon. Its body is bloated, deep orange spilling out across the water, a vibrant rippling beam. I climb up the vacant lifeguard chair, aligning myself with the liquid light. I cross my legs and sit like a child, cheeks glowing as I bathe in the warm light.

I close my eyes and imagine myself for a moment back inside. *How many nights have I let slip away? How many moons have risen and fallen without me seeing?* I open my eyes and look around. I am the only one here. The soft glow draws me in again, palpable and real in the sky but impossible to capture completely in my gaze. I focus in on the details—the burnt shadows of craters and distant landscape.

With a shift of attention, the rounded planet becomes whole, murky in the details but full as a larger image. I can't see everything at once. Still, I try, flipping back and forth between the detailed parts and the whole, just like I used to when I was a kid, lying under the stars in my parents' old sunroom.

Eventually, I rest my eyes, gently closing my lids. My hands gravitate to my thighs, turning over with the palms facing up and open. I breathe in slow and deep, steeping in the moon's calm yet radiant waves. My neck and shoulders straighten as a clog in my head disintegrates and drains. I feel peaceful and clear but also energized and alive. Exhaling, I breathe out the tension and the ache. A cavity rises from my gut and breaks free in the air. Its walls crack and weaken, crumbling away as the void touches the night sky and becomes a part of the nothingness all around. I smile. I've never felt so full. Mirrored and bathed in the blood-orange light, I feel oddly at home.

"Hello!"

I jolt as my eyes flash open. A man below walks by on the sand, turning his head back toward the shore.

"You scared me." I laugh. He looks up again.

"Oh, sorry! I thought you could see me." He waves and continues on. "Have a great night!"

"You too." I gaze as he blurs into the dark fuzzy distance. He and I share this secret. I am not alone. I turn to the moon again, surprised by its faded shade. The pale orange ball sits higher now in the sky, shrunken and worn of its deep mysterious color. I stare and breathe a bit longer. After a while, I decide to go home.

I climb down the chair and walk back to the parking lot to start up my car. The clock reads 9:15 p.m., but the green glow of time doesn't bother me. I unlatch the front of my Jeep's soft top and flip it back, driving slow and looking up occasionally to remember the stars. They're still there. I can see them now, and they haven't changed. The eight-year-old girl stares up through the glass ceiling as I stare up through my car's open roof. Magic exists—it always has. I simply forgot.

Chapter Twenty-Three

My counselor gathers the edges of her shawl and wraps the front of her body as she sinks into the sofa chair. She smiles, breathing me in.

"So how have you been?"

"Good! Really good actually."

I scoot deeper into the couch and lean back, but the angle doesn't feel right. I return to the edge and uncap my carbonated tea. The cool fizz tingles down my throat. My counselor places her steaming cup to the side.

"I can tell. So what's new? What have you been up to?"

My eyes widen as my head nods. "A lot! So many changes over these past few weeks." I screw the cap back onto the glass bottle and place it on the ground. My hands move as I speak. "I changed my diet and started cooking for myself, dropped off two more rocks, started a chakra workshop with my friend Laura—oh yeah, Laura's back! I'm so happy. She and I are on the *exact* same page. We've been hanging out a lot."

My counselor's eyes light up. "That's incredible! I want to hear more about everything." She crosses one leg over the other and leans back. "Tell me about your diet."

"Yeah, definitely!" My back straightens, and I breathe in. "Okay, so basically I had an epiphany the other night—well, not an epiphany. Just a realization, nothing crazy." I cringe. "Whatever, it doesn't matter. Basically, I realized that for most of my life—ever since I was eleven—I have been eating *against* my body: starving, binging, purging, *dieting*. So even though I call this a 'diet,' what I've really done is change my perception on eating." I laugh. "This is gonna sound creepy, but I'm calling it 'eating for my brain.' I researched all the best foods for my body, specifically my mind." I rest my hands on my knees and force a slow breath in. "Food is my medicine. Since I started eating this way, I haven't felt the need to binge."

My counselor's mouth is open, but as she shakes her head, the corners crack into a smile. "You are amazing. I swear. I can't believe you decided to do this all on your own."

I smile and gaze down, remembering the orange glow across the waves. "Yeah. Everything just hit me one night. I realized I was ready for major change." I look up suddenly. "But don't worry. I'm still taking my pills."

She frowns. "I wasn't worried."

My face tightens. Her words aren't true. I wait for the rapid undertones to vibrate across the room, but underneath the silence, the air is calm. My shoulders relax slightly, still ready to brace.

"So tell me about the other major changes. I want to hear about this chakra workshop."

I take a deep breath. "Yes! Oh man, I don't know where to begin."

"Take your time."

She leans back. I gulp down another sip of tea and cross my legs.

"So a couple Fridays ago, Laura and I wanted to hang out but felt like doing something different. I told her about gong meditation." I laugh. "I've been trying a lot of weird new things. But anyway, she's weird like me and seemed interested, so we looked up events like that and came across this introductory chakra class. Long story short, we *loved* the class so much that we decided to sign up for the seven-week series."

My counselor cocks her head, stuck on something as her eyes gently search. I look away.

"I don't think that's weird. I think that's cool."

"Oh. Well, thanks." My thumb rubs against the golden stubble on my knee.

"So each week, do you focus on a different chakra?"

I look up. "Exactly! We just started Monday, so we've only worked on the root chakra so far—the red one."

"And are you in a classroom or…"

"No. That's what Laura and I loved about it. Everybody takes a mat and lies down in a circle. The instructor sits in the middle, and we all close our eyes as she walks us through our bodies. A lot like what you did to me that one time! It's very deep. I had no idea classes like this existed, or that *people* like this existed."

She smiles. "Your tribe."

"Exactly!"

I laugh as I pull my enthusiastic hands back down. I reach for the bubbly tea and gulp. My counselor squints beyond the tilted glass.

"Is that the lavender kombucha?"

"Yes, it's my favorite flavor!"

She laughs softly. "Mine too. Did you ever get the lavender essential oil I suggested?"

"I did! And I also bought lavender bath salts, pillow spray, and a candle. I went lavender crazy!" I laugh and shake my head. "No, but seriously, I feel good. I'm happy but in a relaxed way. I'm not like I was a year ago. This is different."

"You're balanced," she smiles. "And it sounds like this happiness is all coming from you."

"Yeah." The purple label around the bottle lifts under my nail. I rip a small tear.

"Speaking of balanced, how are your other friends?"

I rip off another piece. "To be honest, I haven't seen them in a while, and I don't really want to either." My fingers start another tear. I put the bottle aside. "I'm not isolating though or cutting people off. I know my old patterns. I'm just…"

Her gaze is curious. I look down and sigh.

"I don't know. Ever since I made all these healthy changes in my life, I don't feel like being around my other friends. I'd rather hang out with Laura."

"Why do you think that is?"

I look to the bookcase at the back of the room. The steam from her tea dances in between. "Well, it's like you said. I've found my tribe. Laura understands, but my other friends don't. All they wanna do is drink and meet boys."

"Have you tried doing other stuff with them?"

I laugh. "No. I already know they wouldn't be interested."

"How do you know that?"

I nibble at the soft tissue inside my cheek. Her question digs. "I've had girlfriends like them before. In high school, I called them 'my club friends.'" I return to her eyes. "I've been reading a lot about introverts lately. I don't want to pretend anymore. Now that I'm finally accepting who I am, I don't want to be around extroverts."

The truth sifts out and dangles in the air. I cringe at the exposed bones, but through the dust, my counselor's expression doesn't change.

"Maybe some of your friends feel the same way."

The clouds of dirt disappear. "What do you mean?"

"Well, maybe they're scared too. Maybe they don't want to reveal their introverted side because they're afraid they won't be accepted. I think a lot of people struggle with this."

My neck straightens. "Yeah. That's what I've been reading. We live in a society that shames introverts and forces us to hide. I'm done hiding. I'm done pretending to be an extrovert."

She tilts her head. "You can be both." I watch silently as she leans in. "I hope you don't mind me saying this, but I've noticed you have a tendency to think in black and white."

I pull my head back. My body stiffens as she continues.

"We're all some degree of everything. Your party friends might not be just your party friends, and you may not be just an introvert. I've known you for almost a year now. I've seen your other sides."

The reaction rushes to my mouth, but the words are small and flat. I keep my lips pressed. As the words dissolve like tissue on my tongue, I realize something strange: my counselor has never labeled me. She's never once called me bipolar. I stay within her eyes.

"And I'm sure there are times when you *do* want to do 'extroverted' activities. You don't have to limit yourself. Life is all about balancing the extremes."

I think about my sister. My eyes drift to the side. The contrast between us has always been so clear, but that belief is old. The blank wall below the skylight draws out a timid smile—one I've been suppressing lately, unable to make sense of. I do love concerts. I am excited for the rock festival in the fall. My sister didn't sway me or influence me. The idea was purely mine.

"I guess you're right. I have always thought in black-and-white terms. I never realized there was so much gray."

She smiles. "So what else have you been up to? How's your rock project going?"

My back straightens, awakened by the energy peaking in the mounds of my cheeks. "It's amazing. I'm honestly loving the entire project, and the unburdening trips—holy crap! I feel so empowered and independent."

"How many more rocks have you dropped off?"

"Two. I left the one about anger at the top of Mt. Norwottuck and the one about my mom on the edge of a waterfall."

"That's beautiful." She reaches for her tea. As she takes a sip, I scoot forward and recross my legs, anxious to tell her more. She speaks first. "I'm curious, what's the mom one about?" Before taking another sip, she looks up again. "Only if you want to share. We don't have to talk about it."

I shake my head and ease back onto the couch. "No, it's okay. I don't mind. I've already dealt with the pain and let go."

I sink into the cushion, sloping down in the worn-out fibers. *How many people have sat here before?* The compressed imprint holds their weight, heavy in the stuffing. My head drops as I struggle to form the words. They came so easily when I was alone. Suddenly, the room dims, and I am twenty-one again, in a different office, but on the same couch. I pick at my nails, aware my counselor is changing.

"Um, actually, I don't know if I want to talk about this."

"That's okay! You don't have to."

Underneath her voice, my tears form. I keep my head down as I wipe them away. They shouldn't be here—not after all the work I've done. I clear my throat and widen my eyes, drying them out before I look up. Her brows are scrunched, gaze shiny with regret.

"I'm so sorry we had to end on this note. You can stay a little longer if you'd like."

I look up at the clock. All feelings drain. "No, it's fine. I'm good. Don't worry. It was just a momentary thing."

I open my purse and hand her three twenty-dollar bills. She places the money on her desk and walks back over to hug me.

"Text me if you need anything."

"I will."

I pull away and walk out the door. Beyond her office, the staircase to the exit is steep. I hold the railing as I hurry down, rushing to my car to lock myself inside. I start up the engine, but I don't move. My hands are shaking. I dig through my purse to find my phone—anything to distract from the anger that shouldn't be building. The screen lights up—a voicemail from my sister. I clutch the phone to my ear as her voice spills out:

> Hey, Miss! Um…so I've been thinking. Is there anyone else who would want to go to the concert with you? I've just been working a lot and…

Her voice fades out as the static in my head takes over. She's lying. I know she is. Work isn't the problem—she just doesn't want to go. I delete her message and chuck my phone aside. The tears form fast this time, leaking out before I can clench them away. I look up, jaw tight as the memories swirl back: all the hours I spent listening to her favorite songs, learning about her favorite bands, and caring too much. I squeeze my eyes. So willingly, so faithfully, so stupid and pathetic, I stood out of the frame and watched her dance. I care too much. I drag my nails up my neck over the lumpy veins. I care too much. I care too much. *Why the fuck doesn't she care the same?*

I reach for my tea, but the cup holder is empty. I left the bottle of lavender upstairs by the couch. I look out to the road, watching the cars fly by, willing the static away with each bulleted breeze. My breath steadies. The enflamed tissue clogging my throat deflates. I stare as the road melts into waves, liquefied through my eyes. My sister lied, but I'm lying too. Anger isn't the truth—it's not what I'm really feeling. It never has been. I blink as a tear rolls out, leaving a trail down to my chin. The truth is, I don't know who else to invite. None of my friends know the real me—the whole me—at least none of my girlfriends. I wipe my damp jawline, spreading the unfamiliar cool down across my neck. Another tear falls. I spread it the same.

Chapter Twenty-Four

I turn the key, but my engine won't start. The dark cloud pours down. I try again, holding the key in place as the gears grind underneath the pounding rain, but nothing clicks. *This can't be happening. Not now.* Athena steps forward onto my center console, panting as I turn the ignition again and again. Nothing. I look to my planner and up through the relentless sheets of rain. I have no choice. I have to call my mom.

"Hey, hon! Perfect timing. I just left the gym."

"Mom. I need your help. My car won't start."

"Oh. Do you want me to come—?"

"Yes, please. As soon as you can."

"You got it. I'll shower now and head up."

"Thank you."

I put my phone aside and try the engine again. This time, the rumble clicks. The engine starts. Eyes wide, I turn to Athena. Both our mouths are open.

"Holy shit! Okay. I guess we can go."

I grip the wheel as we drive, a thousand calculations popping up in my head. The clock glows bright underneath the heavy clouds. I'm twenty minutes behind. I turn my wipers up to full speed, the arms moving like a manic metronome. I push further down on the pedal. I can't stop. I can't fall behind. I pull into the driveway of my next dogs' house, leaving the engine running as I rush inside. I leash up the dogs and run out of the door. Athena steps onto the driver's seat, but I push her back.

"Nope. We're going somewhere else today."

I lift the other two dogs inside as they all cram together in the back seat. I jump in and back out the driveway. Athena creeps forward to the passenger seat, her long legs locked and trembling as I shift into drive. I slide my planner out from under her onto the floor and place my hand on her back.

"Sit down, baby. Relax."

Her hind legs resist, so I drive on, breaking slow and turning wide. She stares through the rain, neck low and panting.

At the next house, I park and take the three dogs out. I rush them to the side gate and let them loose in the yard, ignoring the cold drips down my neck as I rush past my unlocked and running car. As I climb the front porch steps, my phone rings. I hurry into the house and slide open the back door, counting the three dogs as they bound past me to join the others in the yard. I unzip my pocket and answer the phone.

"Mom?"

"Hey, I'm leaving now."

"Awesome. Thank you so much. I got my car to start somehow, but I can't shut it off. Call me when you're close."

"Oh, that's great! Should I meet you at the car place?"

"No. I'm still walking dogs. I'll let you know where I am."

I hang up and head out the back door, pulling my hood up over my hat to the brim. I pace around the yard, counting the six dogs: two under the bushes, one jumping beside me, and the other three around the side of the house under the second-level porch. I toss a ball and peek around the gate to my car. The exhaust steams out. I can only see the back end. I rub my jaw and take out my phone. I call the nearest dealership, but they're booked. I bite my nail and call two more. They're all booked too. I pace back and forth, caught between the dogs and my car. Finally, I call my dad.

As soon as the thirty minutes are up, I bring the three dogs back inside and drive the remaining three home. On the way to the next stop, my phone rings again. My mom's here. I look to the nearest street sign and pull over, telling her to meet me there.

In my rearview mirror, I spot the turquoise. My mom pulls up and parks behind me as I jump out. She rolls down the window.

Through the blown-in rain, she squints. "What are we doing?"

"I talked to Dad. He told me to go to the muffler place. They said they can take my car."

"Okay. Sounds good. I'll follow you."

Back in my car, I try to ease my foot on the gas, but the pressure is stiff through my toes. Keeping the blue in my rearview, I focus ahead. My mom stays close. She turns into the shop's parking lot and pulls up beside me. I jump out, moving past her lowered window.

"Want me to come—?"

"Stay here, Mom. I'll be right back."

I jog to the front doors, my hood flapping against my back. I burst inside. The guy behind the counter looks up. I drip across the waiting room, my rubber boots clopping against the linoleum floor. I stop at the counter. The man listens. He follows me out to my car and waits in the driver's seat as I grab my planner and purse. Before shutting the door, I spot my bag of rocks in the back. I hesitate and then yank the backpack out, carrying everything to my mom's car. I drop the bag in her back seat and plop down next to her.

"Mom, thank you so much. You have no idea."

"Of course! That's what I'm here for. Phew though, what a nasty day. When I got out of the gym—"

I open my planner and zero in on my next stop. Her voice rattles the ink, each word jittering under my skin. I rub my neck, trying to smooth out the bugs.

"Hey, Mom, let's get going. I've still got a lot of dogs to walk."

"Oh yes! Where am I going?"

"Head back into town. I'll tell you where to go."

As she pulls out onto the main road, I force a breath in and out slow. I'm not used to her new car. The trucks tower overhead as we fly by. The seat is low. I feel like a child.

"I brought a towel for the dogs. It's in the back seat."

I turn around, wincing as my chest swirls with a familiar sweet sickness. She tucked in the corners. The back seat is neatly covered, smoothed from all wrinkles.

"Thank you, Mom. I really appreciate you doing all this."

"My pleasure! Now should I go straight?"

I look to the road. "Yes. Sorry. And then take a left at that street."

She speeds ahead as I return to my planner. I darken the already crossed walks and lean into the turn.

"Okay, and the driveway is right there. No, right *there*!"

I press my nails into my eyebrow as she backs up, trying to crunch out the bugs. Before she has a chance to park, I hop out of the car. In the foyer window, the puggles bark. I open the door and leash them up, hurrying them back outside as the rain streams down.

"These guys have to go in the car. Is that okay?"

"Yeah, that's why I brought the towel. Do you need hel—oh! They just hop right in."

I brush off the seat and slide back in. "Yeah, they know the routine. Okay." I sigh and open my planner. "Now we need to go to Greenough. Head back down this street and turn right."

One of the puggles steps forward and sniffs my mom's hair. She laughs as she turns to him.

"Aw, they're so cute! What are they called again?"

"Puggles." I scratch my neck and look at the clock. I wait as she pets him. Eventually, the puggle steps back and the car begins to move. I brush the dirt from the center console as my mom slows at the stop sign.

"So how many walks do you have left?"

"After this, the Manchesters with the three dogs on Kane and then Ruby, and then we gotta drive to Portsmouth to walk the pug and then…" I run my finger down the page and check the clock. "Ah, I don't know if I'm gonna have time. After that, I have the cavaliers and then a couple pet sitting stops too…"

She looks both ways and takes the turn. "Wow, busy day. You must be making a lot of money."

My jaw tightens. I open my phone to text the owners of my last three stops, telling them I'm running late. The puggle steps forward again, but I push him back, brushing off the muddy prints.

"Okay, you can park here. I'll be right back."

I jog down the shell driveway and open the back door. Inside, the owner looks up, surprised. She didn't hear my car. The three dogs bark and run toward me.

"Yeah, my car wouldn't start this morning, so my mom's here."

I grab the leashes from the mudroom hooks as the owner gets up from the couch. She points out the front window. "Is that your mom?"

I clip the third leash to the collar and look up. "Yeah, that's her."

"Wow! She has a cute car." She peers out the window again. "Hey, if you don't want to walk today, it's fine. I don't want your mom—"

"No, no, I'm good." I pull my hood over my hat and gather the dogs. "The pups love the rain. My mom's gonna stay in the car while we do our usual routine."

I open the door and follow the three dogs as they pull me down the steps and across the driveway. My mom steps out as we approach the car. The puggles jump out and twist around her. She bends to grab something from the back.

"Mom, stay in the car. I can take them."

I reach for the leashes, but her polka-dot umbrella pops out in between. "No, don't be ridiculous. I'm gonna help." The umbrella dances in the air, pulled by the wind as she steps out from the tangle of leashes. I glance over at the house's front window, aware of watchful eyes. Untwisted with the umbrella steady, my mom smiles. "Okay. Ready when you are."

I lead the way as the puggles trip over the slack in her hand. I grit my teeth. I can't tell her it would be easier for me to walk them on my own. My three dogs and I splash through a puddle as she steps carefully aside. The crawling bugs, the guilt, and the anxiety blend. I thank her excessively to counteract the sludge.

By the time we get to Portsmouth, the owners of my last three stops have texted me. They're home. There's no need to rush anymore. The pug is my last walk, and the rain has finally stopped, but still, I can't shake the tension. My mom leaves her umbrella in the car and walks beside me. Her chatter is constant. I stare ahead, nodding too much, trying desperately to care.

"So I got another Dress-to-Impress package in the mail yesterday! Opening those boxes is always so fun."

"Mhm."

"I'm trying to limit myself and only buy one or two items, but it's so hard! My stylist knows me so well. Everything she sends, I love!"

"Mm. Yeah, I bet."

The pug stops to sniff, so I stop too. In the stillness, the scuttling legs multiply under my skin.

"Your father says I have enough clothes, and he's probably right. I just look forward to those packages so much."

I tug on the leash, forcing the pug to move. "Well, if it makes you happy, then that's all that matters."

"It does! I get a little thrill every time I get the notification that my next fix is coming. It's almost like—oh, where are you going?"

I veer off the road into the woods. "There's a trail here. It's short."

The pug prances around a puddle as I step through with my boots. He zooms back and forth—the way he always does when we enter the trail. I turn back to my mom. Her blue and white sneakers sink in the mud. I cringe.

"Actually, never mind. It's too messy. Let's go back on the road."

We finish the mile route along the pavement and drop the pug off back home. As I open the passenger door, I spot my backpack lumped behind the seat. I breathe in as I open my phone and sit down. No messages. My mom gets in and shuts the door.

"So, is that it for today?"

I hesitate before nodding.

"Phew! We did it. Now we can relax and get lunch. My treat!"

The sweet sickness returns to my chest. "No, it's okay, Mom. You've done enough, and I just bought groceries yesterday."

She cocks her head. "Are you sure?"

"Yeah. Let's just go home. I'll make us something."

She looks down at the phone in my hands. "Did you hear from the car place yet?"

I unlock the screen and check again, even though I know the answer. "No. Nothing yet."

"Well, I talked to your father, and if you need us to pay—"

"Nope. I don't need help." My words are sharp—not what I intended. "Sorry. Thank you again. I appreciate everything."

"My pleasure." Her voice is gentle, powdering the air. As she starts the car and backs out of the driveway, my fingers loosen from my phone. I look to her hand. I want to reach out. I want to hold her tight, but the white specks in the air float up my nostrils and spoil the back of my throat. Too sweet, like sucralose on the tongue. I rub my clammy palms, squeeze, and turn away. I hate myself for feeling this way. *Why can't I just be normal?* I swallow several times, but the taste is stained, familiar like the acidic sweetness that persists long after the chunks.

My mom goes back to talking as I sink lower into the seat. I feel young, small, invisible, and without control. I look up to the steering wheel as I try to push the memories down, but the dark room snuffs out the road. I'm standing in the doorway of my parents' bedroom, staring at my mom alone and curled up. I take her hand, needing her warmth, but her fingers are cold. They were cold on the walks we used to take together too. Mile after mile, just me and her—an ear for a voice but never the same in return. I squeeze away the memories, but the bitter juice seeps back up through my ears. I'm on my parents' couch, alone in the middle of the night. My dad found me. I cried when he asked me what was wrong. I cried because at fourteen, he realized the truth before me. He could see that the bowl in my lap and the crumbs on my face contained something other than food. I watched as he went back upstairs to talk to my mom, but neither of them came back down. I waited with the half-eaten bowl the same way I wait here now. I turn to my mom, watching her meaningless words flake off the surface of her lips. I wait, silently yearning for her eyes, angry and aware of our unspoken code. We don't talk about real things—not since my mental breakdown. Last August, I blurted out the truth—the bottled-up years of silence exploded all at once, too violent and painful for either of us to face. My jaw clenches because I remember. My body burns because I know she remembers too. I lower my head, but the rage can't be controlled. Every word out of her mouth is a lie—a cover-up for the pain brewing underneath. It burns. *How can she not feel it too?* My eyes widen, driven mad by the pretending.

"Stop! For once, please just stop talking! I don't care about your fancy clothes or any of the pointless shit Dad lets you buy. It all makes me sick. Everything about you makes me sick!"

She stiffens. My words stab, but I can't stop. The daggers slice through the air.

"It's so obvious what's going on. I know you. All those years you were depressed, *I* was the one you turned to. *I* was the one who listened. *I* was the one who cared and kept all your secrets, but you've *never* done the same for me. You abandoned me last August, just like you abandoned me five years ago. I would *never* do that to you. I would *never* let them take you away."

My body is fuming. I can see the panic in her eyes—the fearful tears. I turn away to claw at the pressure inside my skull.

"I'm just so angry! I should be over this shit by now, but I can't let it go. Every day, they bullied me. *Every single day* they yelled, 'You're fat! You're ugly! You're a slut!' Do you know how that feels? Do you know what it's like to have your entire school turn against you overnight because of one stupid mistake and then come home to a vacant mother?"

I glare up at her. She keeps her eyes ahead, cheeks drawn, white and frail.

"I know. I'm sorry. I know I messed up, but I'm trying. I don't know what else to do." Her fingers shake as she turns the wheel and pulls off the road into a cemetery. She parks the car and turns to me. "I'll spend the rest of my life trying to make up for those years, but I don't know if you'll ever forgive me." She pauses, eyes glassy. "Sometimes I think you want to hurt me."

An icy wave spreads through my cheeks. I look down. The cold leaks from my ears and tingles down my forearms. I unclench my fists, staring at the slivered-moon indents in my palms.

"I would never hurt you," I whisper, but the words are only half true. A moment ago, in the heat of rage, I did want to hurt her—not physically but mentally. The way I've been hurting since I was a kid.

I look over at her hands, fragile on her lap, thumbs gently touching. Her skin looks so soft. Mine feels wretched and scaly.

"I'm sorry, Mom. I really am. I would never hurt you. I would never hurt anyone. I don't know what's wrong with me." I take off my hat and curl forward, scraping and pulling the follicles of my hair. I'm a monster. Without the screaming steam and the boiling blood, the truth is obvious. My mom isn't to blame. I am the cause of all this destruction and pain. I scrunch my hair and pull harder. "I'm sorry, Mom. I'm sorry. I don't want to be angry anymore. I just want to get past all this. I don't know why I can't move on."

I untangle my fingers from the snarls and scrape up the back of my neck. My nails draw out the tears. The pain is deserved. "I hate that I scare you. I don't want to scare anybody. All I've ever wanted to do is love."

A firm hand stops my fingers and coats my skin in warmth. I look up, surprised to find my mom's outstretched arm. She's looking at me.

"I know you do. And I know you say you would never hurt anyone, but look at what you're doing. You're hurting yourself."

Her eyes stay locked on me as the tension in my fingers slips away. The trails along my neck burn underneath the warmth of her palm. I push her hand away.

"I'm not like you, Mom. I can't tuck everything away and deny. I can't pretend."

"I know. And I admire you for that." She looks to the back seat and tries to lift my backpack. "And I admire you for—oh my god." She laughs. "That's heavy as hell!"

"I know." I peek up through my window. The clouds are thin, milky gray with veins of blue. I wish they were dark. I wish it was still pouring.

"Did you do your hike yet today?"

I look down. "No. And I don't really want to."

"Why not?"

I puff out a breath and shake my head. "What's the point? It's obviously not working. I already dropped off the rock about you." My nails gravitate to the side of my skull, but my left hand catches the habit and pulls it back down. "I'm exhausted. I just want to go home."

Her hand grips my shoulder. I look up. Her eyes pierce. "Let's do the hike. Let's do it together and take life by the balls."

I laugh. "What?"

"You heard me. Isn't that what you always say?"

"Yeah, but it sounds funny coming out of your mouth."

We both laugh. She squeezes my shoulder as her gaze steadies again. "No, but seriously, let's do it. I think we both need it."

Before I can respond, she starts up the car and drives toward the cemetery's exit. She waits as the traffic on the main road roars by. I start to give her directions.

"I know where to go. You don't have to tell me."

My lips seal. She looks both ways and merges onto the road. I straighten in my seat.

"And I hope afterwards, I get to try one of these 'brain-healthy' meals you've been raving about."

I smile. "Yeah. Definitely."

Chapter Twenty-Five

By the time I arrive, everyone's already seated on their mats. I take off my shoes and sneak over to the cubbies to slip them inside. Through the dim light, Laura smiles and pats the open mat beside her. I sink down fast, restraining my rapid breath as I adjust my hat and smile at the instructor in the middle. The soft background music trickles in.

"Awesome. Now that we're all here, I invite everyone to lie down in a comfortable position. You're welcome to use the blankets again. Whatever helps you feel most relaxed."

I glance over at Laura as she giggles and grabs her blanket.

"I never turn down a blanket," she whispers.

I laugh as I grab mine and unfold it over my outstretched legs. I drape the wool corners over my toes and tuck the ends under the socked heels of my feet. Through the cotton, I can feel the sweat. I force myself down as I pull the blanket over the rest of my body, trying not to think about all the dog hair and dirt stuck to my clothes. *Why did I have to hike today? Why couldn't I have skipped it to shower instead?* I grab another blanket from behind and slip it under my head. As I relax my neck and ease down, the lump of hair sticking out the back of my hat hits the pillow first.

"Okay, now that everyone is comfortable, I invite you to close your eyes and sink into your body. Feel the floor beneath you. Allow yourself to release any tension you may be holding."

I pull my hair loose from the elastic and scrunch up the blanket to cradle my head. The contour isn't right. I wiggle and slide down a bit, lying still for a moment before wiggling and sliding up again. Every brush of wool against cotton, cotton against rubber, disrupts the tranquil curtain trying to fall over the room. Everyone else is silent, waiting for the warm heavy drape, but with each rustle, the curtain bounces back up. I grab the sides of my blanket and force my body still.

"Take a few deep, cleansing breaths. Allow the air to fill your lungs and your entire body before releasing."

I breathe in deep, my stomach clenching as the air stretches against my rib cage. The rest of the class continues to inhale, so I hold my breath, abdomen burning. As we release, a fuzzy ecstasy floods up through my inner ears. I breathe in again, more slowly this time. With each consecutive breath, my stomach rises a bit more, rounding and relaxing as a space opens up between my teeth. I rotate my jaw, loosening the hinge, allowing the muscles in my face to melt away to the floor. Skittle-sized rings pepper and expand through-out my body. I breathe deep once more, a gentle giddiness taking over. My toes wiggle, pressing against the blanket's secure ends as the instructor's voice seeps in.

"Today, we are exploring the sacral chakra. This second chakra is located in your pelvic region, the womb space."

Her words tickle like a fine paintbrush, soft bristles swirling around my inner ear. A familiar tingle runs down my spine. My head rolls to the right, cheek and shoulder tucking in.

"The color of the sacral chakra is orange. The element is water. On your next inhale, imagine water flooding your pelvic region, opening up this second chakra. On the exhale, allow the water to flood out, cleansing, healing, reclaiming this space."

I center the back of my head against the blanket again and breathe in deep. The air is cool. My feet fall out to the sides as my hips seem to expand, thighs rolling open. There is no one else in the room. No reason to feel ashamed. I hold on to this vulnerability for a moment, intrigued by its peculiar comfort, and then I let go. My breath drains upward, a current rushing out my nose. My cheeks slip down, pooling to the pillow. The whisper continues to guide.

"On your next inhale, I want you to breathe in orange. Feel this light spread throughout your body. On the exhale, breathe out what-ever color comes to mind, a color that no longer serves you."

Orange. Orange. Orange. I will the color in, but the hue keeps changing. My eyes twitch beneath the lids as I try again, over and over, but the voice moves on.

"Breathe in creativity. Breathe out rigidity."

I can picture the words, but they're coming from my tongue. The air seeps in through my nose, collecting and building in my mouth as I force meaning into the space. I'm doing this wrong. I've lost the substance.

"Breathe in acceptance. Breathe out judgment."

My jaw tenses as the pool beneath my head dries back up into my skull. My lashes flicker—a sliver of light breaking through. I reseal the crack and squeeze out the voice as it flows on without me, but I can't block out the sound. *Slow down. Slow down.* I try again to breathe in orange, but the color resists, and the words fail to soak in. I reject breath after breath, focusing on too much at the same time. They are not good enough. I'm not doing this right.

"Now allow your breath to relax. Let it fade away into the background…"

I fend off the instruction. I'm not ready to move on. My teeth grind, caught between where I want to be and where the voice is already going.

"Return to your pelvic region. What does it feel like? What does it look like? What colors and images do you see?"

Too many questions! The once gentle whisper has become just noise. The tingles have disappeared. My cheeks tighten, drawn upward to the pressure building at the top of my head. I'm thinking too much. I'm trying too hard, but suddenly, the voice falls silent. The background music hums, drawing a heavy felt over my eyes. I watch from the back of my mind as my thoughts grow fuzz, fluffing into nothingness as a blackness takes over. A billion green particles dance and sprinkle like static on a dark screen, awakening the transmission. Gravity flips as the distance between the monitor and I deepens, and the grains of green turn to sand. I'm looking down, toes digging beneath the night air, searching for the warmth below the surface. The incubated remnants of light collect and cave over my feet as I bend down to pack the glowing sand. Behind me, a melon moon spills orange across the water. In front, the corner of a lifeguard chair towers in the dark. I straighten my legs and look up, surprised to find myself sitting cross-legged, eyes closed at the very top. I watch as the wind blows through my hair, remembering the tickle as the wispy ends brush my ear. A voice echoes in the black space above, light-years away. The words are distant and meaningless as I continue to gaze up at the radiant surface of my cheek. In the tangerine moonlight, I look peaceful. As the memory unfolds at an angle above, my mind empties and glows peaceful too.

All at once, the meditative state breaks as my closed eyes flash open at the top of the chair and turn to look down. The movement is sharp—she knew where to look. She knew I was here. I stare up at myself as she looks down, locking me in her gaze. She doesn't smile. She doesn't make any conscious expression at all, yet somehow I feel safe. There is no need to react or change. Despite the sudden awareness of my own body and face, I remain the same. She sees me the way no one ever sees me—the observer in the dark. In her eyes, my invisibility is gone but reflected in her certain face, so is the fear.

A lifetime passes before she turns away, and the moon fades out. The darkness takes over and solidifies close to my eyes. The instructor's voice returns too loud and clear. The black screen splits as my eyelids twitch and crack open. I am back in the room, lying on the mat close to Laura. I hear the ruffle of blankets as the bodies begin to move and sit up. I lie still for a moment before sitting up too.

"Thank you everyone for coming. I hope you enjoyed tonight's class and continue to enjoy the rest of your week exploring this second chakra."

I clear my throat and smile. Laura crawls out from under her blanket and begins to fold, so I lift the wool warmth and fold too. We gather our stuff from the cubbies and silently slip on our shoes before heading out to our cars. She stops by my trunk and turns.

"I had trouble getting into that one. My mind was all over the place."

"Yeah, me too, in the beginning…" I shake my head and look up. "It's hard to relax."

"It is!" She smiles. "We're so similar. I was mostly thinking about dinner and how I wish I ate beforehand."

She laughs, and I laugh too, but the emptiness in my stomach doesn't grumble. I look away, yearning for the orange dream. The glow recedes as I chase after my own face, unable to capture the raw gaze from before.

"I don't know, though. I thought that class was more intense than the first. I think I had a vision. It was strange."

"Really? What did you see?"

I turn back to her. My cheeks bubble, mouth curved up in her eyes. "This is gonna sound weird, but I was looking up at myself in a lifeguard chair. The memory was real—all this really happened a few weeks ago—but instead of being in the chair, I was down below observing. There were two me's." I laugh. "I don't know. It's hard to explain."

"No, I get it! That's so cool. You had like an out of body experience."

"Yeah, something like that." My gaze drips away. "Anyway, how was your week?"

She shakes her head and blows out a stream of air. "Crazy. Lots of family shit."

"Oh my god, me too! What happened?"

"The usual. I just hate going to my parents'. My dad's drinking is out of control, and my mom never says anything about it. The whole situation makes me crazy."

I watch her hands rise as she grits her teeth. Her fingers are curved and stiff, angled in toward her skull.

"You're not crazy. That does suck."

Her claws soften and fall back down. "Thank you. This is why I love you. You get me." She moans and closes her eyes. "Ugh, I just wish I could hang out with my mom. Every time I go there for dinner, I feel this intense need to leave and go back to my apartment."

"Have you ever thought about inviting her to your place? Or going out to dinner just the two of you?"

She tilts her head. "No, but that's a good idea. Maybe I will do that…"

"You should! I mean not 'should,' fuck 'should.'" We both laugh. "You know what I mean. Do what you want, but I highly recommend some one-on-one time with your mom. I did that last Friday, not on purpose or willingly at first, but in the end, it turned out to be just what we both needed."

The wind picks up, lifting the end of her long braided hair. The baby hairs tucked around my ear curl and tickle.

"That's beautiful." She smiles. "What about your sister? How's that going?"

My cheeks hollow as the breeze turns cool. I look down to the pavement. "I don't know. I'm starting to think I overreacted with that whole situation. It's just a dumb concert. It shouldn't have mattered that much to me."

"Fuck 'should!' Remember what you just said? This concert *does* mean a lot to you. I think what your sister did was selfish. Addiction does that to people. I would know. Look at my dad."

I keep my eyes on the ground as my chest grows heavy. I scratch my lower lip, craving the softer memories, but the painful ones pull down. In the cracks of pressed gravel and tar, my thoughts cement. I think about my rage. I think about my sister and my mom.

"Sometimes I feel like a monster. Like my family would be better off without me."

"Hey!" Her voice chops the rope pulling down. My head springs up. "You're *not* a monster. That's obvious to me and everyone who knows you, *really* knows you." She reaches out to cup my left shoulder. I stiffen but remain in her eyes as she continues. "I will always be your positive mirror."

Before I can look away, she smiles and pulls me in. I sigh in her embrace, but not all the way. The trapped breath lingers as she lets go. I step back from her long, slender arms.

"So who are you bringing to the concert instead?"

I hesitate. I didn't expect her to ask. "I invited Marley."

"Really? I didn't think you guys were that close."

"We're not." I laugh and look away. "I don't know. It was kind of my counselor's idea. I'm trying not to be so far on one side of the spectrum, but to be honest, I'm a little anxious about the whole plan now. I haven't drank or gone out with Marley in over a month. Or any of the other girls for that matter."

I follow her eyes as she looks to the building behind me and watches the front door open. Our instructor locks up and turns around, eyes wide as she spots us.

"Oh! You guys are still here?"

"Yeah, we're just catching up." Laura smiles. She waves and turns back to me. "I know what you mean though about the whole 'spectrum' thing. I have trouble balancing too."

She and I hug again before parting ways. I watch her walk around to the driver's side of her car while I stand beside mine. As usual, she looks up to wave once more.

"Good luck this weekend! And remember what I said about the positive mirror."

"Same! I'll always be that for you too."

I get in my car and fiddle with my phone, listening for the rumble beside me to back out and fade away. In the silence, I look out both windows. The parking lot is empty. I am alone. I flick on the overhead light and pull down the rearview mirror, squinting as I look up my nose and check my teeth.

Chapter Twenty-Six

In my side mirror, Marley rolls her suitcase across the parking lot. I chug the rest of my energy drink and smile as she opens the passenger door. Her voice bursts in.

"Heyyy, girl! Ready for our road trip?"

"Hell yeah."

I chug the last sip as she throws her bag in the back, swallowing the tangy liquid fizz. I hold onto the taste, willing the tingles of light to course upward through my veins. Marley hops in the seat, smile glowing, eyes wide. My brows heighten to match her peaks.

"I've missed you! I'm so excited to spend the whole weekend with you. I have so much to tell you!"

"Yeah, sorry. It's been too long. I've been working a lot."

"Same! Same here, girl. Ugh. I can't wait to shower and change out of these clothes. How long is it gonna take to get to the hotel?"

I look down at my phone. The GPS is already set with the address plugged in. Marley leans over to check the screen.

"Damn, girl! Four and a half hours? Well, let's get going! We don't want to miss the bars."

I start up the car and head out toward the lot's exit. I wait at the stop sign as the mall traffic pours in. Marley reaches into my cup holder and rattles the empty can.

"Oh, I actually bought another. Hold on."

She smiles. "You did? Aw."

I reach behind to unzip the duffel bag and dig underneath my pile of clothes. At the very bottom, I find the can. I hand it to Marley and glance up at the space in traffic. The driver holding up the line flashes his lights and waves frantically. I jolt through the line of cars and continue onto the highway.

"So what's new, girl? I haven't seen you in forever!"

I merge onto 95 as two eighteen-wheelers roar by. Muffled underneath the banging metal and wind, the GPS speaks. I strain to make sense of the noise.

"Not much. I haven't gone out in a while. I've been super busy. What about you?"

"Me too! Oh, except last night. I was out until 5:00 a.m." She laughs. "Whoops!"

I keep my eyes forward as I join her amusement. She turns and the volume increases—her laughter always persists mine. I can feel her brilliant stare, shining like a spotlight, draining my right side.

"Well, if you want to take a nap, feel free. It's a long drive."

"What? Girl, you know me. I'm good. I'm ready to go out and listen to some rock music with my favorite girl!"

My chest sinks, melting in to a sudden warmth. "Thanks for coming by the way. I know this isn't really your type of music."

"Are you kidding? I love Papa Roach!"

"Really?"

"Yeah, I used to listen to them all the time! 'Cut my life into pieces…!'"

Rouge bubbles over my face as she sings their most famous song. Everybody knows those lyrics—I've heard them mocked a thousand times. Still, I'm flattered even though I know she's pretending.

"We don't have to go for the whole festival tomorrow. I really only care about the last two bands."

"Whatever you want to do, girl, I'm down! As long as we don't end up in a mosh pit."

I smile. "No, no, don't worry. We have seats."

Her spotlight dims as my own softer beam dilutes through. I forgot how funny she can be and how much she cares. My left hand loosens from the wheel as the other slides up, natural into place. The hairs on my arm rise, drawn toward Marley.

"So guess who's been blowing me up lately."

The hairs stop. "Who?"

"Adam. I knew that boy would come crawling back. Listen to these texts."

My skin tightens as the artificial light fills the car. The truck in front of me slows, so I check my blind spot and speed around. As she reads, traffic increases, the twilight road glowing red.

"'I can't stop thinking about your sexy body,'" she reads. "'I want you so bad.' Like, are you serious? This guy is *married*. I was like, honey, you lost your chance. How 'bout you think about your wife!"

"Did you really say that?"

"No. But listen to what else he said…"

I breathe in as I look at the clock: 6:30 p.m. Beside me, the phone is blinding. I lean against the window away from the bleached light, my fingers pressed and rolling the muscles in my jaw.

"And remember Bobby? Yep. He's been texting me too!"

I ease off the brake, inching close to the red glare. Still absorbed in her own LED bubble, Marley doesn't notice. As she talks, I click open my own phone, squinting as I check the GPS. I sigh and dim the screen.

"'Oh, baby, I miss you. Nobody compares to you. I think about you every night. I think about your—'"

"Mars, would you mind putting the address in your phone? Sorry, mine's about to die."

"Oh yeah. Of course!" Before plugging it in, she looks up through the windshield. "Whoa. Where'd all this traffic come from?"

"I don't know. Stupid rush hour."

I push my jaw away, forcing myself up. As I straighten in my seat, she cracks open her energy drink and types out the address in her phone. Gulping the liquid down, her eyes widen at the screen.

"What! Now it says we're not gonna get there until 11:30 p.m.!"

I cringe. "Yeah, I know." I peer over as she checks for an alternate route, highlighting the map's various veins. I can feel the slight shifts in my own body—the meager attempts to stay on course. I glance behind her at the neatly packed suitcase and a small paper bag on the floor. I didn't notice the bag before. She must have slipped it in. My chest tightens at the various heels inside.

"I'm gonna check what time the bars close." I grab my phone. "Maybe they stay open later in Philly than they do in Providence."

The brake lights ease in front of me as I begin to search. I keep my phone open as we begin to move.

"Honestly, I wouldn't mind just staying in and drinking tonight."

"No, Marley. Don't worry. We're gonna make the bars."

Up ahead, a car sits broken down on the side. As soon as we pass, the traffic breaks. I speed up, eyes forced away from my phone.

"Oh, you're right! Some do stay open later. But seriously, I wouldn't mind just—"

My car dings. I look to the dashboard. "Fuck. I forgot to get gas." I switch lanes and pull off at the next rest stop. "Sorry. I'll be quick."

"No, it's okay. I'm actually pretty hungry. Do you want to stop inside and eat dinner?"

"Yeah, we could get sandwiches and eat fast."

I park at the nearest pump and jump out. I unscrew the gas cap and put the nozzle in, clicking the loose handle over and over as I wait for the gas to flow. The handle finally resists. I squeeze, watching the numbers roll up too slow on the screen. I breathe in and look around. I don't recognize the building, but the lot and surrounding trees haven't changed. I shake my head and open the door.

"Marley, I just realized where we are."

"Where?"

"My hometown." I laugh. "I can't believe I didn't notice until now."

"No way! That's so funny. Wow! I'm glad we stopped here."

The pump clicks, so I pull it out and screw the gas cap back on. We drive to the parking lot to find a space and walk up the ramp together. The concrete slope and glass doors are all new, but as we stand in line to order our sandwiches, I peer around, wary of familiar faces.

"What are you getting?"

"Huh? Oh, I don't know. You can go first."

A space opens up between us as she moves in front of me and starts pointing out the ingredients through the glass. She makes her way down to the register as I wait for the second employee to notice me. My back burns, exposed. I watch Marley dig through her purse, a distance away, as the second employee finally looks up. I order the first sandwich on the menu, keeping my eyes down on the cutting board as I follow the open bread. A hand slaps my back. I turn around, relieved to find Marley.

"I'm gonna get us a table."

"Okay."

I straighten my shoulders as I watch her confident stride. I hand over the money and grab the plastic bag, breathing in deep as I cross the room and join her at the table.

"So what about you? Any *boys* in your life?"

I slide the dressing-soaked package from the bag, peeling off the paper. A man walks by. I keep my head down.

"Huh? Oh…no, not really. I'm kinda taking a break."

"What! Girl, you said that last time!"

I take a small bite of the bread exposed and begin to chew. Marley watches. I swallow the tasteless texture and wipe away the excess dressing from the corner of my mouth.

"We've gotta get you *laid*!" Her voice is loud. She tears open her own sandwich and opens wide. Even though I'm not hungry, I chew fast, body curling in. In this bright fluorescent light with my elbows cold on the table, I eat for show. I eat to get this meal out of the way so we can return to the car.

"I don't know how you do it." The meat and cheese muffles her words. "I *need* sex. It's so important!"

Laughter carries from the far corner of the room. I turn, but I don't recognize the faces.

"Are you okay?"

I turn back to Marley. "What? Yeah, no, I'm fine."

She lowers her sandwich and stares. "If this topic makes you uncomfortable, we could talk about something else."

"No, it's not that." I shake my head, turning to the dark window beside me. The beams stream by in the distance. My face softens as the lights lure the stiffness away. "Or I don't know. Maybe it is." I breathe in and turn back to her, expecting to find her lost in her phone. My chest opens. She's still watching. "Can I be honest with you?"

"Yes! Please."

I put my sandwich down and clasp my hands underneath the table. "This isn't a phase for me, this whole no-guy thing. I've been in relationships since I was thirteen. I'm trying really hard to be okay on my own."

"I totally get that! But your body still needs love! You can still hook up with people, right?"

"No, I can't!" She leans back. I breathe in and lower my voice. "Sorry. It's not you. It's this place. I really hate being here."

"Do you wanna leave?"

She starts to wrap up her sandwich. I sigh and look around.

"No, no, it's okay. I don't want to ruin our meal. I just need to relax."

"You're not ruining anything. Come on."

She grabs both our sandwiches and gets up from the table. I begin to follow, but halfway to the door, she turns around and waits for me. I catch up to walk next to her out to the car. Inside, we close both doors.

"Okay, so what happened? What's up with this place?" She pulls up a leg, her hip curved, and turns toward me in her seat. Underneath the soft glow of the lamp light above, she reminds me of the moon. I breathe in slow, milking her warmth.

"Well, I think I might have told you once when I was drunk."

"You mentioned you were bullied, which I still don't understand. I don't know why anyone would ever bully you."

I look away. Nobody ever believes me. Nobody ever understands.

"What did they do? I mean, why were they picking on you?"

I tap my mouth and look back. Her lips are so full, hair short and curled in pixie tassels. She radiates femininity.

"I don't usually tell people this, but I lost my virginity when I was thirteen."

She nods silently, so I continue.

"The guy I lost it to broke up with me a week later, and then he told the whole school. That's when everything changed. I lost all my friends, and people I never knew before started calling me a slut. I went from being unknown to 'the girl who got fucked.' Even at home, they found ways to harass me."

"Holy shit! Why didn't your parents take you out of that school?"

"Because they didn't know. I tried to keep everything to myself. Actually, maybe my dad knew…"

She shakes her head. "Wow! I can't believe you never told me." She breathes in and sighs. "So what happened to the guy?"

I laugh. "He became the most popular kid in school, of course."

"That's so fucked up."

"I know!" I laugh again and look out the windshield toward the sky. "Oh, life! You gotta love it. You *have* to love it." Smiling, I turn back to her. Her face is somber.

"I'm sorry you went through that."

"No, don't be sorry. I'm actually happy that all happened. Everything I've been through has made me stronger, or at least has helped me understand others on a deeper level."

She looks down and purses her lips to the side. Her leg folds up from the floor, back curved in like a crescent.

"Well, since you're being so honest, can I tell you something?"

My chest rises. "Yes! Anything."

She takes a deep breath. "You know how Nick and I have been together for a long time?"

"Yeah. Eight years, right?"

She nods. "Sometimes I feel…trapped. Guilty too because I really do love him, but we're so…different. He never touches me. He never even holds me or plays with my hair."

I breathe in slow as I watch, the air heavy but brand new. My lungs fill with the rich substance. The hairs on my arm start to rise again. She looks up, so I lean in, wanting to hug her—wanting to tell her she's safe.

"Have you talked openly about this with him?"

"Yes! A hundred times. We've tried everything! We even considered couples therapy."

I smile, puffing out a breath. She tightens at the sound. "No, sorry, I'm not laughing at you. I was laughing because I've actually been there before with an old boyfriend. Same reason too."

"Really? Did it help?"

Her rounded eyes glisten. I want to turn but I can't look away. "To be honest, no, but every situation is different. It could work for you guys."

She nods fast and closes her eyes. "No, I kind of already know it's not gonna work. I'm just so afraid to leave him. We've been together for so long." She breathes in deep and smiles, reaching out her hand. "Thank god for girlfriends. I don't know what I would do without you girls."

I watch as she unravels my clenched hands and holds them separate within her own. The automatic part of me wants to pull away, but instead, I squeeze harder. Remembering her need to be held and my desire to hold, I gather her hands together, sealing them within my warmth.

"You are not alone. You can always open up to me."

She smiles. "You too."

The aroma of baked bread and salty meat suddenly awakens my nose. I shift back in my seat as she bends down to pull up the bags. She hands me my sandwich and presses the button on my radio to check the time.

"Woops! I guess this was more than a quick stop."

"Shit! I can eat and drive." I start up the car, but her hand stops my arm before I can shift into drive.

"You don't have to rush. I'd rather stay in the hotel and hang out with you tonight, if you don't mind."

"Really? No I definitely don't mind."

She lights up. "Yay! Now I'm even more excited! No need to shower too." She unwraps her sandwich and takes a huge bite. I smile and do the same.

"Hey, do you mind if I plug in my phone?"

I look to the aux cable dangling in her hand. "No, go right ahead. Play whatever you want."

I take another bite and breathe in slow as I chew. Suddenly, the music cuts the air. My jaw stops as my heart beats knowingly to the sound. I turn to Marley and smile, watching as she nods her bouncy curls offbeat to the heavy percussion.

Chapter Twenty-Seven

I push the branches aside, moving fast through the trees. I have no idea where I'm going, but at this point, I don't care. The rocks on my back clunk with each step. I pull the tabs tighter on my shoulder straps as a dangling leaf tickles my cheek. I rub my face. The woods shouldn't be this green. By now, the leaves should be turning, but the air is stubbornly warm. Another branch reaches out, but I snap it in half and throw the limb to the ground. My head drops down as I begin to count.

"Root, dirt, stump, mushroom."

My neck strains from the weight on my shoulders. I grip the straps, squeezing hard as my mind continues to race. I shouldn't be surprised. I knew after this weekend, I'd still be hungover. The swirling and restlessness is all chemical—it isn't real—but I know this is only partially true. I walk faster as my skin lifts and begins to crawl. A rock slips past the inner lining and thumps freely against my lower back, but I can't stop. The rhythmic nuisance pounds, beating me back into my body with each thud. I rub under the brim of my hat and search for more objects as the headache grows.

"Beetle, grass, poison ivy, dog shit."

The technique is useless. I groan and close my eyes. *What am I doing? Do these hikes even matter at all?* I squeeze and open my eyes. Ahead of me, the path splits. I stare at the map nailed to the tree, but the shapes and colors blur together—they don't mean anything. I step over a cluster of roots and veer right. I don't care if I get lost. These woods may be new, but my thoughts are painfully old. I barrel ahead. I shouldn't be here—not after all the work I've done.

The heat builds, trapped inside my hoodie. I pull the zipper down, just a few inches of relief, as my sweat stains the air. I cringe. I can still smell the alcohol. My stomach gurgles as I move—yesterday's binge sloshing around. I tighten the waist strap, squeezing in my belly to choke out the sound. *What would my counselor say?* I already know. Her words are useless in my mind:

> *All feelings are innocent.*
> *Stay in the moment.*
> *Ride the waves.*

All day yesterday, I repeated these phrases too. I ran a bath, but the water got cold, so I let it drain and returned to the kitchen. I shivered as I opened the fridge. There was nothing left. I paced around, looking at my phone before finally giving in. Staring at the clock, I counted down the minutes for the doorbell to ring and the food to arrive. I couldn't wait though—forty minutes was too long. I grabbed a bowl and poured in the sugar, spooning in mouthfuls of crystals, rotting out my insides.

My teeth grind as I hear Marley's voice again. She was laughing yesterday morning as we drove back home.

"When you drink, it's like you become a different person. It's like a demon takes over!"

I tried to laugh with her, but I couldn't find the humor. She talked about the night as if I remembered everything, but after the concert, my memories only came in bursts. I squeeze my eyes, trying to focus instead on the loose pounding rock, but one by one, the rock knocks back the scenes. With each thud, the reel of film rips and changes. *Rip.* I turn and see Marley's face. She's staring behind me at the line of powder on the bathroom sink. *Rip.* On a stranger's bed, I lean over in the dark, searching for a condom. There was none. I fall back asleep. *Rip.* Lying on the same bed, the daylight hits my naked skin as the strange man opens me up. He sees my inner thigh and suddenly looks up. "Did you do this?" I quickly cover the scar. *Rip.*

I groan and shake my head. My legs rub together as I move, burning out the memories in between. *Where was my self-control?*

Where was my strength? A thorny bush tugs at my sleeve and drags across, catching and tearing as it jumps to the mesh pocket on the side of my backpack. The elastic snaps free, hitting the bag like a rubber band shot from across a classroom. I pull the rocks up and hunch over, looking to either side through the trees. *Is this all just a joke?* The dangling nuisance on my back taps incessantly—an insulting, torturous sound. *Am I a mockery of my own condition? Am I really just a fool?* Leaning forward with my head down, I watch my big feet, remembering the man on the cover of the magazine with the rocket strapped to his back. Maybe the doctors were right. Maybe I am bipolar. Maybe I am promiscuous, impulsive, reckless, and obscene, and there's nothing I can do about it because the problem isn't strapped to my back—it's unchangeable inside.

I force my head up as the trail angles down. My stomach growls again, but I ignore it as I reach the bottom of the slope and trek up the next hill to a wall of pines. The trail extends out to my sides—a straightaway of fallen needles in both directions. I turn left, moving fast, pretending I know where I'm going as the tunnel of dark green draws me in.

Insects buzz. I swat the sound and rub my ears, but the static is coming from somewhere else. I listen to the steady ring as the shadows on the ground darken—black like the venue in between sets. In the midst of the crowd Saturday night, Marley glowed, but not in the same way I was. She was on her phone, texting someone, so I looked down and pulled out my own. *Why did I have to do that? Why did I have to miss him?* A rock trips me up as my vision stumbles back to the trail. Between the tops of the trees, the strip of sky is gray, obscured by the clouds. *Where is the relief? When will I start to feel whole on my own?* The line containing the gray cracks open as a small dirt path leads me off the main trail through the pines. I follow it down to a sandy clearing on the edge of a lake. The pool of ink floods my mind, cool and calming as I watch its secret stillness pull me in. I sink down on the edge of a stone wall, wincing as the loose rock in my bag clacks against the surface. The weight on my back pulls and the straps dig in as I gaze out across the lake, so I loosen the tabs and breathe, allowing my stomach to grow. The wind blows through the leaves on the other side, whipping little peaks across the dark liquid glass. I watch the water tickle toward me, looking up to find a figure standing in the middle of the water. He isn't real. My eyes narrow as he smiles and beckons me in. A storm inside me begins to rage.

I stand up and unclip my backpack. The vibration from the weight as the bag hits the ground fuels the building heat. I toss my hat aside and pull loose my hair, unzipping the hoodie and tearing my arms free from the sleeves. I rip off every last piece of fabric and deceit from my skin, dropping it all to the ground until there's nothing left to shed. Naked, I walk out to the lip of the lake, keeping my eyes down, ignoring the mirage in the distance. The water trickles over my toes and cools its way up my shins. When it reaches my waist, I breathe in deep and lie down, my head held above the surface as my body floats below in a diluted, rusted world. My limbs begin to sink, disappearing into the depths as the air seeps from my lungs. I watch the wary shadows as the minnows move in, picking at the dead skin. My body lies still. I'm not afraid. With one last breath, I cover my ears and let go, allowing the water to splash over me and coat my closed eyes. I lie underneath the liquid skin, cradled in the deep as the visions and memories finally fade. There is no hunger, no regret, no yearning, no pain. Submerged at the bottom, there is no mirror—only fish food and silence. I open my eyes and push up, breaking through the blackness. In the middle of the lake, the reflection of Steve is gone. I search all around, but I am alone.

Chapter Twenty-Eight

The Manchester terriers are standing up in the back, watching the houses blur by as I speed down Valley Road. I look at my planner, gritting my teeth at all the uncrossed stops and optimistic allotted times. *What was I thinking?* My foot eases off the pedal as I drift by the police station on the left. I'm already running late, and I still have eighteen minutes of driving before I reach my next stop. I never should have said yes to this job in Tiverton.

A few cars ahead, the light turns red. I nibble on the inside of my cheek and tap the steering wheel as I inch closer to the bumper in front of me.

"Come on, come on."

Through the rearview mirror, the driver glares. I push down on the brake and look away to my passenger seat. Lying face up, my phone flashes silently. I lean in to the name on the screen and smile. I pick it up without thinking.

"Steve!"

"Melissa, hey, it's not good." His voice is cold, stiffening my spine.

"Why? What's up? Are you okay?"

"I need you to take me to the hospital."

"What?" The light turns green. I hesitate forward. "Steve, what's going on?"

Through the silence, his breath is unsteady. I move across the lanes, turning left to loop back into Middletown in the opposite direction from where I need to go. His voice returns, small and strained.

"My dogs are in the car. One of my client's dogs is in there too. They won't let me leave. They—" His voice trails off as I pull off the road. I ease into a parking space, mind solid and still. I close my planner and toss it on the floor.

"Okay, okay, where are you?"

"I'm at the VA Clinic." His tears unravel. "They're making me go to the hospital. The same place you—"

"Where's the VA Clinic?"

Silence. My neck strains forward, detecting a faint sound. There's someone in the background. I straighten as the receiver crackles into clarity.

"One Corporate Drive. They said you can't come here, though. What am I supposed to do with my dogs? They won't let me leave."

"Steve, don't worry about it. I've got the address. I'll be there soon."

"It doesn't matter." His mumbles trail off.

Before I can respond, he hangs up the phone. Leo steps onto the center console, but I push him back and tip up the lid. I text the owner of the Tiverton dogs to let her know I'm running late. I type the address for the clinic into my phone and pull back onto the road. The GPS says I'm three minutes away.

"In five hundred feet, turn left onto Corporate Drive."

I look back before easing into the left lane. I breathe in, forcing the air out slowly as I sit beneath the red light, hands gripped on the steering wheel. My phone flashes on my lap—Steve's calling again. I pick it up, hand shaking.

"Hey, I'm almost there."

"They're not listening to me. They won't let me leave."

"I know, I know. What room are you in? Do you know the number?"

"No…I don't know. They won't listen to me."

"Okay, it doesn't matter. I'll figure it out."

The call ends suddenly. I sigh and look up at the light. My body burns underneath the red's steady glare. One of the dogs whines in the back, so I turn around. They're both sitting side by side, small noses pointed, staring at me with their shiny brown eyes. My cheeks soften as their faces cool the scalding tension.

"I love you, guys. I'm sorry this is happening."

Cary's tail wiggles. I turn back around. The arrow is green, so I crank the wheel left and accelerate down the street and into the entryway on the right. I don't see Steve's car, but the GPS tells me I've arrived. I circle the enormous building, its concrete windowless walls like a fortress. On the other side, opposite the road, I spot the white Subaru. Inside, three dogs turn their heads and stare. My heart rate speeds up. I pull into the space next to the dogs and park quickly. I rush over to Steve's car, my hand on the window.

"I'll be right back, guys, I promise."

His two dogs wiggle with excitement in the back seat, but the black lab seated in front only stares. He doesn't know me. None of them understand what's going on. Behind me, the Manchesters bark. They paw at my back window.

"I promise, I'll be right back for all of you. Just stay here."

I look back and forth between the cars as I back away. My ribs squeeze as the clouds above begin to spit rain. I turn around, pulled toward the building but split in half from behind by the two abandoned cars. I open the front door. My rain boots squeak across the hall's linoleum floor. There's no front desk. Only three shut doors. I open the one on the left to find a small waiting room with a row of vacant chairs. I walk in and move toward the sliding glass window on the far wall. The secretary doesn't notice me, so I wave. She slides open the window.

"Can I help you?"

"Yes, I'm here to see Steve Goodman. He's somewhere in this building, but I don't know exactly where."

Her brows lower as she looks me up and down. A drop of rain slides down my cheek. She turns to her computer as I wipe the streak away and swallow. Her fingers clack across the keyboard and then her hand moves to the mouse to scroll.

"I don't see Steve Goodman here." She looks up. "Who are you?"

"I'm Melissa Toni. I'm his friend. He called me and asked me to come here."

She purses her lips to the side and returns to the screen. "Have a seat. I'll see what I can do." Her hand reaches up and slides the window shut. I step back and turn toward the chairs to sit down. The metal frame is stiff and cold.

I gaze around the room, counting objects to distract myself from the tension, but as I run out of objects, the strangling grip in the air increases. I pull out my phone. *Two missed calls from Steve.* I call back, cringing as the ring pierces the silence. His voicemail clicks on. I hang up and text back instead:

I'm here.

Breathless, I wait for his response. Nothing comes. I sigh and look up to the sliding window, eyes wide as I bite my nails. I just want someone to tell me what the hell is going on. I rip off a sliver of dead skin and flick it to the ground. I tear at another, trying not to think about Steve—trying not to think about the dogs or my schedule either.

Suddenly, the door to my left bursts open. A nurse stands over me.

"Can I help you?" I peer behind her as the door slowly closes. My chest lifts. I can see a hallway and several curtained rooms. Steve's in there. I know it.

"Yes, I'm here for Steve Goodman."

"He can't see anyone right now. May I ask how you know him?"

I clear my throat as she crosses her arms. My shoulders begin to hunch, but I roll them back into place.

"I'm his friend. He called me. I'm here to help with his car."

"We'll take care of his car. You don't need to worry about that."

"Yeah, but there are dogs in there. We're both dog walkers. He needs someone to take them back home."

She stares for a moment and then sighs. "Wait here." She disappears back through the door.

I look to the secretary's window again. Through the glass, I can see her talking to another nurse. They're standing close together near an open door. Someone else rushes down the hall behind them.

A burst of air hits my back. Three cops pour in from the back door, moving fast, their armored bodies shake the room. One glances down as he rounds the corner, but he looks away as he follows the other two through the second door. They pile into the long hallway, vanishing right into the first curtained room.

I open my phone to text Steve, but our conversation is still frozen, stuck on the last message I sent. I groan, rolling my head up to the ceiling and back to the closed door. My fingers pick, digging up pieces of flaky skin. Behind the glass, the secretary watches me. She's still standing with the other nurse, but they're both looking at me. They turn away to continue talking, their voices silent behind the soundproof glass. I scroll through my contact list, mindlessly. I just want someone to tell me what's going on. I need someone to talk to. The clock on the wall ticks. The sound is maddening. The second hand seems to move slower and slower as the intervals clash with the racing beat in my chest.

The door to my left opens. My head shoots up. *Steve.* His face melts to tears as I stand. I hold him as he crumbles in my arms. His shoulders tremble under my chin as the pain bursts out. I absorb it all, the uneasy waves rolling down my back.

"It's okay, it's okay."

The three cops and a couple of nurses trickle into the room. I close my eyes, leaning into Steve's shoulder and away from their presence. His tears are hot—they saturate my skin. I hug him closer, my arms long, enveloping him. We feel equal in size.

"It's okay. Everything's going to be okay."

He continues to cry, but the waves aren't as fierce. Still, my arms are locked, prepared to hold him forever if that's what he needs. I peek open my eyes as one of the nurses turns away. Lined up along the wall, the cops look around the room, hands resting on their holsters. One of them glances up. He seems familiar. I close my eyes again, hiding from their discomfort and hiding from my own paranoia. I don't care about their feelings. I don't care if any of them know me. I don't even care to know why any of us are here. All I want is to keep holding Steve and make whatever pain he's experiencing go away.

Eventually, his head lifts, so I release my embrace as we both pull away. His eyes are red, cheeks puffy, but the melting has ceased. His mouth hardens into a straight thin line as he runs his hand through his messy hair. Heat flushes my cheeks. I turn away and pull out my phone, keeping my eyes on the screen.

"I need the black lab's address and the owner's number."

Steady now, Steve's voice deepens. Under his breath, my fingers begin to shake. I can feel the whole room staring. I hold my phone closer with both hands, trying to mask my nerves. As Steve reads the phone number, my finger slips and messes up twice. He sees. He takes my phone and types the number himself. My body shrinks. He hands back the phone as I stare dumbly at the screen. I feel small.

"Okay, are you guys good? Does she have everything she needs?"

I shake my head and force my gaze up. "No wait, Steve, I need your keys."

He digs through his pockets and hands me his car key. The cops begin to shuffle out as one of the nurses escorts Steve through the back door. Left alone with the remaining nurse, my cheeks cool. She moves toward me, face gentle but restrained.

"Steve will be staying at the Newport Hospital for a few days. We don't know for how long, but—"

"I know. I've actually been there myself."

Her eyes widen for a moment and then they relax. "Oh, so you already know the routine."

"Yep." I shake my head slowly and smile, exhaling through my nose. "Us dog walkers, we're crazy people!"

She laughs, but as my words confront me in the air, they stir up a repulsion inside. My eyes drop to the floor. She moves close.

"People are crazy. It's the animals that keep us sane."

"Yeah." The air is heavy. My mouth droops. I look up to find her observing. I move toward her and open my arms. "Thank you." I back out fast from the hug and shake my head. Before she can say anything, I turn away and exit the building.

Ignoring the pings of rain, I splash through the puddles, moving fast toward the cars. The dogs haven't moved. They're all still waiting, necks extended, eyes big staring out the back. I unlock my car first, scooping the Manchesters out from the back and walking them across the pavement to the patch of wet grass along the far side of the lot. As they sniff and prance along, I pull out my phone and call Erin. I listen to the ring as I look back at Steve's car, flipping his key around in my hand. I don't know what I'm going to say. I haven't exactly thought all this through.

"Heyyy."

My eyes widen. "Erin?"

"Yesss."

"Hey! What are you doing right now?"

"I'm in Connecticut at work. Why? What's up?"

"Oh shit, okay, never mind."

"Why? Are you okay?"

"Yeah, yeah, I'm fine. I'm just in a bit of a situation." I look down at the Manchesters as they finish peeing. I tug on the leashes and begin walking them back to the car. "I'll figure it out, though. I gotta go. I'll call you later."

"Wait, no! You gotta tell me what's going on."

I open the door and lift the Manchesters into the back seat. My mind is spinning. I don't have time to explain, but the tone in Erin's voice is the same as mine was earlier. I can't leave her wondering. "Steve just went in the hospital. He's fine—he's gonna be fine—but right now I have a bunch of—"

"Steve's in the hospital? What? Why?"

"Honestly, I don't know, but I'll keep you updated. Right now, though, I have to figure out what to do with his dogs. I'm sorry. I gotta go."

I hang up the phone as I pull out Steve's key. Inside his car, I start the engine and plug the lab's address into my GPS. I back out of the parking lot and merge onto the road. As I drive, I try calling my other friends, but nobody else picks up. I breathe through the lights and veer left off the main road, hurrying down a side street. The GPS urges me the other way, but I ignore the voice, forcing my phone to reroute. As I join up with another main road, a line of cars stands solid underneath a red light. I close in on the line, slowing to a stop, but as I press the brake down, the car falls silent. The light turns green, but his car doesn't move. The gas pedal does nothing.

"What the hell is happening?"

I crank the wheel right, drifting slowly off the road. The momentum isn't enough to carry me to the side. Steve's car sticks halfway out, blocking the road as cars pile up, beeping from behind.

"I know! I know! Something's wrong with this car!"

The three dogs watch silently as I throw the car into park and scramble frantically for the hazard lights. I give up on the search and turn off the key. I try flipping it on again and the engine rumbles.

"Oh, thank god."

I wait for the angry drivers to rush past before pulling back onto the road. I check the GPS and then call the black lab's owner.

"Hello?"

"Hi, is this George?"

"Yes. Who's this?"

"Hi, my name's Melissa Toni. You don't know me, but I'm a friend of Steve Goodman's. He had an emergency today, but Steve is going to be fine, and I have your dog. I'm calling to let you know I'm bringing him back now—"

"Wait, what? Is Noah okay? What happened?"

"Everything's fine." I hold my phone out in front to check the GPS and then put it back up to my ear. "Noah and I will be back at your house in three minutes. You're at 1041 Poppe Drive, correct?"

He sighs. "No, that's the gate code. The address is 143. Did Steve give you that number? Is he okay? What's going on with him? I just saw him yesterday."

My phone beeps with an incoming call. "I'm not sure, but I have the right address now. I'll talk to you in a few minutes."

I end the call and pick up the other line. It's Marley. At the next stop sign, I slow, looking left and right past Noah's big head before rolling through.

"Hey, Marley."

"Hey, hon, what's up? I saw your missed call."

"Yeah, are you busy right now by any chance?"

"Well, I'm at work, but I could talk for a bit. It's slow today. It's been so boring here with no customers and all the rain—"

"Gotcha. Okay, never mind. I'll text you later."

As I hang up, I cringe, but I have no choice. I toss the phone on the seat next to Noah, bumping his leg. He looks at me and then down at the phone as the GPS announces we've arrived. I park in front of the locked gate and jump out to punch in the code, the mismatched numbers still clear and ready in my mind. As the hinges creak, I hop back in the car and sneak through before the gate has a chance to fully open. The gravel slides under the tires as I brake fast to park. Noah stares. I reach around him to the floor, digging through the empty seltzer cans and discarded clothes. I pull out two leashes.

"Okay, um, crap which one's yours?"

He continues to stare. I throw the red one back on the floor and clip the purple one to his collar. I lead him out of the car and across the driveway to the porch steps. George is standing at the top.

"Is this your leash?"

He shakes his head. "No, but that's okay. What happened?"

I sigh as he grabs the leash. Noah turns around and sits next to George. They both stare at me, waiting for me to speak.

"Honestly I can't—I don't know. I'll text you as soon as I know more though. I do have to g—"

"Did something happen with his dad? He mentioned something about his dad last week."

One of Steve's dogs barks. I turn back toward the car. Waves rip under my skin.

"I honestly don't know, but Noah will be covered in the meantime. Here's my card. I'll text you details and options for next week by tonight."

"Next week? Is Steve hurt? Did something happen while he was out with Noah?"

"No, don't worry. Noah wasn't involved, and Steve is going to be fine. I'm sorry. I really have to go. I'll text you later."

I turn and hurry back toward the car, ignoring the fog of unanswered questions left hovering behind me. I start up Steve's car and peel up to the locked entrance, tapping the wheel as I wait for the iron gate to slowly swing back open. Once through, I speed down the back roads, taking the quickest route to Steve's apartment. I park outside his building and rush the dogs up the stairs, moving too fast for the memories. I round the staircase to the third floor and stop to open his door, but the knob doesn't turn.

"What the hell?"

I jiggle it a few times and step back. The dogs push their noses up to the crack, desperate to get in.

"No. No. He never locks the door. Why's this happening?"

I push the dogs aside and bend down to look under the mat. Nothing. The metal rack behind me is cluttered with tools and boxes. I search underneath and around, fast and then slow as I remember something. Steve walked me out once and reached up above his door.

This won't ever happen, but in case my door's ever locked, I keep a spare up here.

I spin around and run my fingers across the top of the frame. Nothing. No key—just dust. I breathe in slow, eyes wide.

"Okay, okay, I got this. I'll just take the dogs with me."

I pull them back down the stairs and into the car. Once back at the VA Clinic, the dogs' tails drop silently as I park in the same space as before. I crack open the windows and shut off the car.

"I'm sorry, I'll be *right* back."

I get out and stand between the two cars for a moment, considering my options, but as the Manchesters begin to bark, I realize I have none. I can't put them all in the same car. They'd never get along. I leave the Subaru behind and get in my Jeep to drive the Manchesters back into town.

Ignoring the green glow of time slipping by, I park in front of the Manchesters' house and lift them to the ground. Their paws patter rapidly as I hurry, key ready in hand, to the front door. I push the key in the lock, but it turns without a click. I open the door to find the owner already home, seated inside at the dining table. My body freezes, but I force a smile. I bend down to take off the dogs' harnesses, fingers shaking as I try to act natural and move slow.

"How were they?"

171

"Good! They were great." The words spill out too fast. Free from their harnesses, the dogs scatter. I gather up their leashes and fumble to hang them on the hooks.

"Where did you guys go today?"

I double the leash around the hook but the weight of the harness pulls down the slack. I bend down quickly to gather the mess.

"We went to Tiverton. We walked with two new dogs."

The back of my neck burns as I continue to fiddle by the hooks. I can't look at him. I wish I could tell him the truth. I wish I didn't have to lie.

"Oh, where in Tiverton?"

"Um…" My mind is blank. I try to picture the name of the street, but all I can see are the two dogs still waiting for me. They're looking out the living room window, ears perked by each passing car. I can't remember the address or any of the buildings nearby. All I can see is my planner and the list of unchecked walks I still have left to do. I pull my lanyard and car key over my neck and turn around. "It's um…out past the marina. It's a ways away. That's why we took a little longer today."

His gaze is calm—observant and still. I look down at one of the dogs as he trots by.

"Okay, guys, well have fun with your dad. I'll be back Monday!" I wave to the owner and start to leave, but he holds up his hand to stop me.

"Wait! You forgot your check."

He slides the check off the table and hands it to me. My face burns as I reach out and grab it. "Thank you."

His eyes are gentle. They dig deep and stop me for a moment, asking me questions I wasn't even aware of asking myself. I turn away and walk out quickly through the door.

Back in my car, I drive slow as I retrieve Steve's dogs and continue my day. The dogs pant in the back, so I stop at a quiet intersection to roll down both windows. As I lean back across the passenger seat, I notice my phone. Marley's name lights up the screen. I consider picking up, but instead, I toss the phone back on the floor, and this time, I lay my planner on top. The call goes to voicemail as I make my way up to Tiverton.

By the time I finish the rest of my walks and make my way over the bridge for the night, it's 10:00 p.m. I haven't eaten since breakfast, but I'm not hungry. I take the overnight dogs for a quick walk before sneaking Steve's dogs inside to the guest bedroom where I shut the door. The three of us crawl into bed where I pull out my phone and begin responding to the mass of messages that have built up over the course of the day. My thumbs tremble over the screen. Even though I'm lying down, I feel like I'm still moving. My skin tingles, irritated and restless. I breathe through the agitation, trying to empty out the lingering energy. Unable to relax, I slide up to a seated position and text fast. I reach out to the owner of the overnight dogs, and then I respond to all my friends. In the middle of explaining my day to Laura, a strange 401 number interrupts the screen.

"Hello?"

"Hey." The voice is solemn and deep. It's Steve. "I don't know if you saw, but I texted you my contact li—"

"I got it. I did see. I was actually just about to write up a message to send to your clients—something generic, nothing personal, just like the message my mom sent out to mine a year ago."

He sighs, a pressure valve released. "Thank you. I knew you'd know what to do. How were my dogs?"

"Good! Noah was fine. I brought him back home, and I actually have your dogs with me right now." I laugh as I stroke the top of Harley's head. She rolls over and stretches out her front legs. "A bit of a crazy day for all of us, but we're good. Your apartment was locked, so I had to bring them with me to this house in Tiverton. Don't worry though. Everything's fine."

"What? Why was my apartment locked?"

"Don't ask me! But it's all good now. You don't have to worry about anything. I'm keeping your dogs separate from the ones I'm sitting because I know how Harley can be."

He sighs again. "Thank you. You're seriously the best."

"Yeah, of course! How are you doing?"

"Well, you know. You've been in here. It's pretty awful how they lock you up and take everything away. I went to the clinic for help. I wanted to start seeing someone. I had no idea this would happen. I didn't know they would send cops to my apartment and have them search through my stuff. I never should have left that stupid note out."

My hand stops petting. The jittery beads under my skin tighten and freeze. I wait for him to speak.

"Oh my god! It was the cops!"

"What?" My voice is small.

"The cops! They must have locked my apartment. Ahh, well anyway, they only let me keep my phone long enough to write down a few numbers, and then they took that away too."

I shut my eyes, remembering the gray phone in the empty hall. I only had two numbers memorized, but the line just kept ringing. My mom and my sister weren't picking up, and I didn't know my dad's number. My lip twitches, but I rub the nerve away.

"That's good. I'm glad they at least let you write down some numbers. They don't usually do that…"

"Yeah, I guess. It just sucks. This system is so messed up."

"I know."

Harley's arm stretches out further toward me. I take her paw and press the rough pad to my cheeks, slowly patting across my face. I rest her paw against my forehead and hold it there, lowering my head to close my eyes. "I'm coming to visit you tomorrow." I open my eyes. "I mean, as long as that's okay."

"Yeah…yeah, that would be great! I didn't even know people could visit me here."

"They can during visiting hours, but the nurses don't make that obvious. Those visits kept me sane. I know how important they are." I drop Harley's paw and lift my head. "But yeah, anyway, I'll be there. I can bring other people too if you want. Just let me know."

"No, don't worry about that." He pauses and takes in a breath. "My girlfriend doesn't want to talk to me right now, let alone see me."

My cheeks flush. I hold the phone slightly away.

"Oh shit, I'm sorry. I didn't know."

"No, no, that's okay. It's a weird situation. Not everyone understands."

I listen, lips thin. I wait for more, but nothing comes. The silence grows thick. Just above my stomach, the frozen beads begin to stir. They jump sporadically, uneasy waves moving up my esophagus. I swallow and clear my throat.

"Okay, well, I'll plan to be there at one. Just try to relax and get some sleep tonight. I've got everything covered here."

We say goodbye, and I hang up the phone. Immediately, the walls of the bedroom swell, bloated and pulsating with the blood beating through my veins. I press my hand to my chest, trying to contain the powerful pulse. I don't trust this energy. The ripples are wide, uneven and fast. My mouth curls up, but I shake the sensation away, leaning my head back toward the ceiling. The popcorn surface swirls lower. I look desperately toward the window, my throat constricted, unable to breathe. I throw off the covers and press my nose against the cool glass, gazing up at the moon. Its soft milky glow washes over me. My breath fogs up the glass.

I turn around, surprised to see myself standing across the room, staring back at me through the vanity mirror. I'm half naked, legs bare wearing nothing but my underwear, an oversized T-shirt, and a pale face on top.

"Get your head on straight. You can do this."

I crawl back into bed and curl into a ball beside my phone. I finish my text to Laura and then stare at the screen, watching the three dots sprinkle up and blink beside her name. Eventually, her response comes—long and sincere. I read through her text, scrolling to the bottom as her final sentences seep in.

Just be careful. Don't get too caught up.
Remember to take care of yourself.

I stare a moment longer, rereading the words, and then I click out of the conversation to move on to Steve's list of clients.

Chapter Twenty-Nine

Sitting across the street in the visitor parking lot, I pull down my rearview mirror. I check my teeth and push the mirror away, pulling it back down to check again. *Why do I care? I shouldn't care.* The corners of my mouth twitch. I wipe my wet palms over my jeans and look to the brick building in front of me. The hospital towers above. I take a deep breath and open my door, walking fast away from my faint reflection on the side of the car.

Through the hospital's front doors, a shiver runs up my spine. The air is cold, infected with the residual powder of latex gloves and medicated fibers. I hold my breath as I approach the front desk and attempt a smile. The woman looks up but doesn't smile back. My lips are weak.

"Can I help you?"

"Hi, yes. I'm trying to get to the eighth floor."

I speak too loud—too fast—but her face doesn't change.

"The elevator is down the hall to your right."

"Thank you."

I hurry to the elevator and press the button to go up. As the chamber makes its way down, my heart races. I pull at my sweatshirt's sleeves and the stitched bottom of my tank top underneath—anything to distract from the weighted cavity sinking in my chest. The gears click, and the hum stops, but the metal doors are still closed. The smooth silver reflects. I resist the urge to turn sideways—the way I turned a hundred times this morning in my full-length mirror. My figure splits in half as the door cracks open. I step inside and press the eighth floor, closing my eyes as the walls seal and the rumble of machinery takes over.

What am I doing? Why am I back here? The questions sift up from the floor, disturbed by the monstrous vibration. The elevator stops suddenly—too early. I step aside as the door opens, and a cart pushed by a man in scrubs rolls in. I flash a smile and look down to my phone, keeping my eyes on Erin's text as the elevator rises again:

> Sorry I couldn't come with you today. I left a gift
> on your porch for when you get home.

My thumbs hover over the screen as the elevator stops short again. The man pushes the cart out, disappearing around the corner. I stuff my phone back into my purse and press the button to close the door, holding my finger there until I reach the top.

Like a curtain on a stage, the doors slip away, revealing a scene I should recognize—a scene I should fear—but the white wall evokes nothing. I drift around the corner and down the hall, floating toward the first of two locked glass doors. I reach out and touch the handle, surprised my hand doesn't simply pass through. A nurse walks by beyond the second barrier of glass. She spots me and turns, snapping me back into the boundaries of my body. My heart is pounding. A violent energy races through, arresting my thighs, trapped and trembling at the knees. The door buzzes as the lock clicks and the handle drops down in my clasped hand. I push and walk through, forcing my body forward to the second door. The nurse stares at me through the glass and points to my purse. I lift it up and start to unzip, but she shakes her head. She speaks through the intercom.

"You have to leave that in the locker."

I turn to my right and stare dumbly at the grid of metal doors. I open the nearest locker and stuff the purse inside. I turn the key to lock the door. The nurse stands still, waiting for something. She leans into the intercom again.

"And take the key with you."

"Oh."

With the sharp metal gripped in my hand, the nurse buzzes me in. She watches as I step inside, cornering me with her clipboard.

"Name and name of the person you're visiting."

"Melissa Toni. And I'm here to see Steve Goodman."

She scans her finger down the clipboard and flips to a second page. A patient at the end of the hall suddenly appears. He glances over—young, baggy clothes, shaggy hair—and then disappears into one of the bedrooms. I clear my throat. The TV and voices creep around the corner from the common room.

"Okay, you're all set. Just sign in at the window down there."

The nurse walks away, leaving me stranded on my own. I glance down the hall. Steve hasn't seen me. I could still leave. I could turn around now—make up some excuse—and he would never know I was here. From the open bedroom, the shaggy-haired boy emerges again. A nurse appears by his side and hands him a small paper cup. She waits as he swallows the pills and rubs his eyes. He retreats slowly to the dark bedroom again as I look down. I can't leave—not yet. I move down the hall, my breath shallow and my legs resistant. At the window, I pick up the pen and turn. *Steve.* Tucked away in a small alcove with the phone to his ear, he sees me. I wave, but he only lifts a couple of fingers. I turn to the sign-in sheet, writing slowly, following the curves of the ink as I try to steady my breath.

"Hello."

A hot flood pools down my face. I turn to the voice, close over my shoulder, to find Steve red-eyed and ashamed as he looks down. The heat drains from my ears. I wrap my arms around him and hold onto his surprisingly small frame, the way I did yesterday.

"Thank you for coming."

"Of course!" My shoulders rise as I step back. The skin around his eyes is puffy, but I try not to notice. I lead him to the common room. "Come on, let's go sit down."

He follows quietly as I walk him to the couch. He sinks down on the edge, beside the armrest. I look to the nearby sofa chair, but I don't sit down.

"Do you want water or anything?"

He glances up. "No, that's okay."

"All right, well I'm gonna get some. I'll be right back."

I walk to the kitchen and grab a cup. I fill it from the faucet and return to the common room, ignoring the "No Food or Beverages Leave This Area" sign. I sit down on the sofa chair and angle my knees toward Steve, sliding back a bit to retain some distance.

"How'd you sleep?"

He clasps his hands together in his lap, rubbing his thumbs over each other. "Okay. It took a while to fall asleep, but eventually I did."

"Yeah, this place isn't very relaxing." I look around and take a sip of water. "Do you have a roommate?"

"No. They gave me my own room." He smiles slightly. "The one thing that's kind of nice about this place is the view. I saw the most beautiful sunrise this morning."

I smile. I remember thinking that too. The surface of the water in my cup stills and bleeds to violet with a ruby underline. When I was in here, I couldn't believe what I was seeing. I woke up the other patients so they could gather around my window and see the beauty too. My hand trembles as the colors ripple away. I thought I was going home that day. I close my eyes as I remember the nurse who took me aside. *Soon.* The maddening word hits me again.

"That is one nice thing." The words drip into my cup. I breathe in and look up at Steve, widening my eyes. "So your room must be on the other side."

"Yeah, but I mostly hang out in here. It's lonely over there."

"Good!" Steve jolts and looks up. I lower my voice. "Good. That's awesome. I'm glad they're letting you out here with the other patients already."

A nurse appears around a pillar and walks behind the couch. She makes her way to the end of the craft table, eyes discreet as she surveys the room. I wait for her to disappear and then I lean in close to Steve. He leans in too.

"Keep doing that," I whisper. "The more you socialize, the faster you'll get out of here."

He nods his head. I glance around and continue.

"You'll know you're getting close when they move your room to this side. Have you been going to the group meetings?"

His eyebrows scrunch together as he looks down. His finger taps against his lip.

"I met my psychiatrist this morning. I haven't heard anything about group meetings…"

"Oh, that's right. I forgot they don't have them on the weekends." I sigh. "Well, on Monday, when they start up again, go to as many as you can."

His eyes are locked on mine. "Okay. I will."

I blink and shift in my seat, realizing my body. I roll the rigidity from my shoulders and soften back into place.

"What did your psychiatrist say?"

He looks down at his lap to clasp and fiddle with his hands.

"He didn't say much. We mostly talked about pills."

"Did they put you on any?"

"Abilify." He looks up. "Is that the one they gave you?"

My face freezes. "No…well, yes, but not recently."

"Which one are you on now?"

Scrubs shuffle behind me. I turn. A nurse peers over her clipboard at me as she walks by. I turn back to Steve. He watches me too but in a different way. I can't lie. His eyes are so wide.

"I actually stopped taking mine."

"You did?"

He leans in closer, elbows resting on his knees. I recoil from his laced hands jutting out toward me.

"Yeah, but I did it with my counselor's help. My parents know too. I told everyone."

"How long ago? I had no idea."

His eyebrows are low, the way they flatten when he's deeply listening. I look down and bite at a piece of skin on my lip. Steve cocks his head. I peel off the rubbery remnants as he enters my gaze.

"A little over a month ago. But like I said, I've got support. You don't have to worry." I look up suddenly. "And please, don't let my decision affect you. Everyone is different. I do think I needed pills to help me through my darkest times."

He breathes in and nods slowly.

"Yeah, this is definitely one of those times for me." He looks down—black hair cow-licked and thickened with grease. He smiles and puffs out a laugh. "You and I had very different reactions to darkness."

I rub my thumb across my bottom lip, feeling the rawness from where I peeled.

"Last September wasn't my first time in a hospital." My voice is barely audible. "When I was twenty-one, I became depressed too."

I look up carefully. His gaze is gentle and deep. An unexpected calm warms the room. I want to seep in, but as my knees graze his knuckles, the warmth flashes red. I need to stay in control. I need to stop talking and remember my role.

"So what else is going on? How are your friends?"

He sighs.

"I don't know. Honestly, you're one of the only people who even knows I'm in here. Besides my girlfriend…"

I keep my eyes steady. "Do you feel close to your friends?"

"Not really. All we ever do is drink."

I laugh. "Yep. I know what you mean." The cup of water rises to my lips—a familiar habit, but the taste isn't the same. As I sip and stare, I realize something strange. This is the longest sober conversation Steve and I have ever had. I've never seen him so clear. "It's a learning process, that's for sure. My friends and I are just starting to realize there are other things to do."

"Like what?"

I look out toward the window across the room. "Hike. Talk. Work on healing." I breathe in and sigh. "I'm finally learning it's okay to be vulnerable, to not be perfect." I smile, remembering Marley's words. "For so long, I thought I had to hide and keep up this fun, outgoing persona, but turns out, it's okay to be myself. It's okay to make mistakes."

I turn back to Steve. His brows are flat again, mouth small. I watch his secrets trickle out as his lips part slightly.

"People always say I laugh a lot, that I'm too loud, but that's not the whole me. I'm not always like that."

I lean in. "Well, you don't have to pretend anymore. Turns out you can be exactly who you are, and good friends will accept you fully."

He smiles. His fingers unclasp as one hand reaches out toward my knee, but he doesn't touch.

"If I had known there were visiting hours, I would have come to see you too."

I laugh, leaning back as I shake my head. "Hell no. I wouldn't have wanted to see you." My words come out harsh, slapping him across the face. I cringe at the pain. "I mean, we didn't even know each other. I was a complete mess. I didn't want to see anyone."

He smiles slightly. "Yeah, I guess you're right."

Suddenly, a girl twirls into the room behind the couch. Steve turns and laughs as she pulls back his shoulders and runs her fingers through his hair. The bun on her head flops loosely as she talks.

"Oh my god, I can't get over this hair! Doesn't Steve have the most beautiful hair?" She looks at me but doesn't wait for an answer. "I keep telling him he's going to be fine. I mean, look at this face! How could anyone this handsome be sad?"

She cups his cheeks and squeezes. I stare blankly as Steve continues to laugh, trying to figure out if I should intervene.

"Looks have nothing to do with that," I mutter, too soft for anyone to hear. The girl spikes his hair into a Mohawk and rushes around the couch to face me on the other side. I shake her hand.

"You must be Steve's girlfriend! It's so nice to meet you."

I pull my hand back and stiffen. "Oh, no, no, no, I'm just his friend."

"What? No way. Steve, how is she not your girlfriend?"

Steve's face is still red, lit up with laughter from his rounded cheeks to the tip of his spiked hair. The girl continues.

"I mean look at her! *I* would date her."

I cover my face as she steps a few feet back into the center of the room. She begins to dance, swiveling her hips to the imaginary beat. I laugh. I don't know what else to do. She points at me.

"You! You probably know how to dance. I want to learn. Am I doing it right?"

"Yeah, you're doing it. I think you look good."

"Really? You think so?"

She pulls her hair loose from the bun and spins around. As she dances, the frizzy brown waves bounce and flip off her shoulders. I look to Steve. We're both laughing. I don't remember anyone acting this way while I was in here. The girl pivots and stops suddenly, facing Steve.

"Seriously, though, screw your girlfriend. You should be dating this girl."

My face hardens. "Okay, that's enough. We're seriously just friends. Steve has bigger things to worry about anyway. He's gotta focus on healing."

She twirls again, ignoring my words. Steve's continuous laugh fills the silent gaps, but I hold onto the space as I stare. I catch her eyes, and she stops. Her smile drains.

"Okay, okay, I'll leave you two alone."

I watch her as she walks away, and then I turn around to look up at the clock: 2:30 p.m. A half hour left.

"Do you have to go?"

I breathe in as I look at Steve. I know I should leave, but his gaze is soft again. The glow from his cheeks has faded and the crest of hair on top of his head is starting to separate. I close my eyes as I remember my mom. She never looked at the clock. Every day until the last possible second, she always stayed. I exhale and open my eyes. Steve looks so young.

"No, it's okay. I'm gonna stay."

The hospital walls expand out of view as a bubble forms around us. We talk without interruption for the remaining time, forgetting time altogether until a pointed pen pops the illusion, and the nurse responsible tells me it's time to leave. Steve walks me to the front and opens his arms for a hug.

"Thank you for everything."

"Of course." I relax from his arms and step back. "Like I said, I know how important these visits are. I'm free tomorrow. Do you want me to come back?"

He smiles. "Yeah. Yeah, that would be great."

"Okay. Awesome. I'll see you tomorrow, same time."

A nurse buzzes me out. I grab my purse and leave through the second door. As I make my way back down, a fuzzy warmth fills my cheeks. I try not to give in as I pass by the front desk and hurry out to the parking lot, but once inside the safety of my car, the sensation seeps through. I can't hide from my smile. Still angled down, the rearview mirror reflects my glowing face. *Stop it*. I push the mirror away and call my mom. She picks up on the first ring.

"Hi! I've been so worried. How'd everything go?"

I scale the hospital's brick wall and close my eyes. "Good. Yeah, everything went surprisingly well actually."

She sighs. "Oh, thank goodness. Your father and I are so relieved. He's right next to me."

"Hi, honey! You're on speakerphone. Mandy's here too."

"Hi, Miss!"

I smile wide. "Hi, guys! Aw, it's so good to hear everyone's voice."

"Yours too, sweetie. We're so happy you're out of there. How's Steve?"

I nod my head as I breathe in. "Not bad. Better than I expected. We had a lot of really good talks."

"That's good, Miss." My sister's voice is far away. A rumble takes over the speaker.

"Are you guys in the car?"

"We are. We're on our way to—"

"We're headed to Grandma and Papa's," my mom interrupts. "They invited us over for lunch."

"Aw, how fun! Tell them I say 'hi.'" I pause, picturing my sister leaning in from the back seat. "I miss you all."

"We mi—"

"We miss you too!" my mom interrupts again. I laugh. I can't help it. In the background, I can hear my sister laughing too.

"All right, well I gotta go, but I love you, guys."

"Love you too!"

I tuck my phone away and glance up to the eighth floor. The warmth tingles down my face as my family's voices fade, and the guilt from above sets in. I start up my car and head home. I rush up my porch steps and stumble as I trip over a package in front of my door. *Erin.* I bend down to pick it up. Folded neatly inside the small white box, I find a pair of wool socks and a note hidden inside.

"Darn tough socks for a darn tough friend."

I place the cover back on the box and head upstairs. I leave the gift on my coffee table and open the drawer, pulling out a pen and an index card to get straight to work.

Chapter Thirty

I walk through the automatic doors of the hospital and smile as I pass by the front desk. I don't need help today—I know where I'm going. I press the button for the elevator, tapping my thumb against the book in my hands as the numbers tick too slow above the metal door. I look down at the handwritten index card on top of my book. Even though I just wrote the list of quotes last night, the words seem meaningless. I've reread them too many times. The elevator door slides open as I slip through. I press the button for the eighth floor and breathe deep as the door seals shut, and the chamber begins to rise.

All night and all morning, I thought of Steve. The book, the index card, and the rock in my hands are the gifts I've settled on, but I had about a hundred other ideas. I breathe and close my eyes. I can't decide if the floors are moving by too fast or too slow. My lips shake as I exhale.

The elevator stops and the door opens. I step through and veer right—no choice but to move forward as a nurse behind the locked door ahead spots me through the window. She buzzes me in.

"I'm here to see Steve Goodman."

Clipboard in hands, she stands guard. She squints and then nods her head. "I think he's working out with some of the other patients. I'll let him know you're here."

She turns away too quickly, a gust of her perfume slapping me in the face. I watch the back of her head disappear around the corner, the same way so many did when I was in here. I haven't forgotten the days I spent waiting for my laceless sneakers, the hours I spent hoping someone might approve. I haven't forgotten the pain I felt watching the other patients return sweaty and satisfied while I paced desperately, up and down the hallways, trying to escape the restlessness and torture of time. The jealousy stirs, but I push it down. I busy myself with the items in my hand, squeezing the rock hard in my fist.

"Melissa!"

Steve barrels around the corner and hugs me. His body is warm and pungent. I'm overwhelmed by the mixture of feelings.

"Sorry, I was just working out with some of the guys. I didn't know when you were coming."

"I told you yesterday." He doesn't hear me.

"What's this?"

I look down at the items in my hands, feeling dumb. I had an explanation to accompany each gift—spent all night and morning rehearsing—but I've forgotten the words. I hand over the pile of stuff all at once, simply saying they're for him.

"Aw, thank you." He smiles, holding my gaze. He turns his attention toward the heart-shaped rock as I suddenly remember what I wanted to say.

"That's labradorite. It's supposed to bring creativity and magic into your life. I bought it a few weeks ago but thought you might need it more than me."

"Interesting." He runs his thumb over the rock's smooth curves. I swallow and quickly point to the other stuff in his hands.

"I also made a list of quotes for you. It's all positive inspirational stuff. And I thought you might like this hiking book. It's about New England trails, super light and easy to read. I wanted to give you something you could flip through because I know how hard it is to concentrate in here."

"Thank you, but actually, I've been getting a *ton* of work done in here. It's so nice to have all this free time!"

My lip twitches. I force a smile, but the corners of my mouth are weak. I remember the tremor on the page as I struggled to read the same word in the same sentence over and over again. Hours dragged on as I sat up in my bed, failing to read.

"And you were right. They moved me to this side today. Let me show you my new room!"

He whips around and heads down the hall. I follow carefully, leaving some space between. When he reaches the open door, he pokes his head inside.

"Hey, roommate!" He giggles and turns to me. "I have a roommate now."

I wave timidly. The boy inside is lying on the mattress with one arm propped under his head and the other resting near an open magazine. He's lying where I had lain. He's in the same bed.

"Steve is the best," he says.

"No, you're the best!"

I watch them both laugh: Steve loud with his head back, and the boy casually, reclined on his side. I should feel happy—happy that Steve seems better and is acclimating so well, but I can't escape the sludge building beneath my skin. It's been two days. *Two days.*

Steve leads me into the kitchen and pulls out a chair for me to sit. He strolls over to the counter and peels open a banana.

"Want anything? Fruit? Coffee? Tea?"

"Um, just tea."

"Do you want milk? Sugar? They've got honey!"

"No thanks. Just plain."

"Coming right up!"

I watch him bounce around as he puts together two cups of tea. The nasty heaviness from before evaporates. A painful cavity in my chest opens instead, sucking in the room, the air, Steve, his two paper cups of tea and his eager smile. I want to hug him. I want to hug myself. I want to sprint down the hall and disappear from this pathetic place, but at the same time, I want to wrap myself around this moment and never leave. There is no one else in the kitchen—just me and Steve. He sits close beside me and hands me my tea. His knee rubs against mine.

"If you want anything else, just let me know."

I nod my head, tipping the cup to my lips. The water is lukewarm. Steve picks up the rock and looks it over.

"What was this called again?"

I swallow the tasteless tea.

"Labradorite."

He outlines the rock's shape as I pick at a hangnail. My cheeks burn. I'm hoping he can't sense the heat.

"You're awesome."

His face is too soft. I prick holes in the air, breaking the silence with questions about his night, how he slept, his family. Regretfully, I ask about his girlfriend.

"She and I actually broke up last night."

"What?" The reaction bursts out of me, sounding too close to a laugh. He looks away as I gain composure.

"Yeah, it was for the best. This whole situation was too much for her. She couldn't handle it. She was fun, but we never really connected on a deeper level."

He looks up at me, his eyes like headlights in the dark. I can't move. Even the smallest muscle twitch could come out wrong.

"I'm sorry." My words are run over by the commotion coming from behind. Two young guys enter the kitchen.

"Oh, hey, look who it is," the blond one says. Steve lights up.

"What's up, what's up!" He laughs. I lean back as they clap hands together across the table. The dark-haired one hangs back and looks at me.

"Who's this?"

"This is my friend Melissa. She's here to visit me."

"Friend? I thought this was your wife," the blond says.

"Yeah, the way you guys were talking just now, you both seemed crazy connected."

The boys both stare, flipping back and forth between me and Steve. Steve smiles and reclines in his seat. I shake my head.

"No, no, we're friends. I'm just here to support Steve."

Eyebrows raised, the blond one frowns.

"Damn, I wish I had friends like that. Steve's the man!"

He reaches out to slap Steve's hand again and then follows the other boy to the table next to us. The dark-haired one squints. He sits on the opposite side of his table, facing us.

"So how did you guys meet?" the blond asks, straddling the bench.

Steve puffs out a quick laugh. He half smiles at me and then leans in toward the boys.

"Well, it's kind of a funny story. We were supposed to have dinner at a friend's house about a year ago, but then I found out Melissa ended up in here, so I told our friend, 'Uh, I don't think she's coming to dinner.' So we didn't *actually* meet until after—"

"Wait," the boy on the far side interrupts, "*you* were in here?"

My face feels cold, frozen. "I was, but—"

"She was but for *totally* different reasons!" Steve laughs loud. I stare, but he doesn't see me. "So yeah, we had a bit of a crazy beginning, to say the least. And now here we are again! Roles reversed. Life is nuts!"

"Oh my god, stop." I cover my face with my hands. An older man walks into the kitchen. He grabs a juice and joins the boys at the other table. He doesn't seem to mind the tension in the room.

"Steve's a good guy," he says. "You should date him. You two would make the perfect couple."

This sets off Steve. His delight is infectious—unavoidable as his booming voice fills the room. A smile creeps across my face, but I'm angry because I don't know who it belongs to. I keep my head down. Everyone's looking at me.

"Maybe one day." My voice is barely audible, but it's enough to make the kitchen explode. A small match in a combustible room. *What have I done?*

"She said yes! 'One day'—that's a yes!"

"Oh shit! I knew you weren't just friends."

The abundance of sound is disorienting. Steve has his head back, laughter bubbling out of him like a fountain. The older guy talks excitedly to the blond, looking at him but pointing at me. I wish I had a jar to contain everyone. The only other person who seems as confused as I am continues to squint. Underneath the chaos, the dark-haired boy asks me a question. I'm the only one who hears.

"I stopped eating and sleeping," I whisper. My head is down. "I was delusional. I was confused."

Half the room goes quiet. Steve didn't hear me, but several feet away, the two boys did. The dark-haired one gets up from the table, leaving the old man and the blond behind, and stands in front of me. I look up.

"Did you start hearing and seeing stuff too?"

I nod my head.

"I've been there. It's amazing how quickly our minds start to change when we lose sleep."

His eyes are sincere. Their depth tells me everything. I begin to breathe again as I listen to him speak. Steve is quiet now, listening too. The boy continues.

"You're lucky you ended up here and not somewhere worse. No sleep can make you do and say things you never would normally. It's scary."

My eyes trickle down. I gravitate toward the back wall, through the paint and plaster to the solitary rooms behind. I'm trapped inside, screaming again, crying and banging on the glass to be heard. Nobody came. Nobody could hear me. It was as if I didn't exist.

"I thought the world was ending," I say to no one in particular. "I thought the devil was real, and everyone I knew was dying. I couldn't stop calling 911."

"You remember that?" Steve asks. I turn slowly to him, eyes glazed.

"I remember everything."

I retreat to my lap. There, I find my hands, lying limp, unable to move. I'm shrinking inside, coiling up fast into a ball. Steve's arm thumps against the table. The sound surprises me. He's leaning in close, neck dipped low, angled toward me.

"You don't have to go back," he says.

For a moment, there is no pain. There is no sadness, no guilt, no anger, shame, or memories at all. His words surround me like a beautiful shroud, protecting me from all thoughts of the past, but the moment doesn't last. The veil is absorbed, and the fabric sharpens within. I wiggle my fingers, blinking away the film from my eyes until the kitchen comes in clear. The boys have left. The old man throws out his crushed box of juice and leaves too. Steve and I are alone again.

We fall back into our conversation from before, discussing the need for deep connection to people and nature alike. I tap the hiking book and tell him about my favorite trails, and he listens well, sharing some of his own philosophies. Time passes outside of us, just like it did yesterday. I jump at the clamber of dishes as two nurses roll in a cart from behind. Eyes wide, I look to the clock. The nurses start to call out names.

"Oh my god! Why didn't anyone tell me visiting hours were over?"

The old man from before walks by. "Now you're trapped."

Steve laughs, but I only tremble. I get up quickly, bumping the table with my hip. The cup of tea wobbles. Steve grabs it before it spills.

"You can take this with you. It's practically full."

"No, that's okay."

"Are you sure?"

I take the cup from him and move toward the sink. I dump out the water, fumbling for the tea bag as it drops into the drain. Steve reaches around me, taking the empty cup. He cleans up everything and then guides me to the exit.

"I'll see you soon." I release from his hug. I cringe at my careless choice of words, but he doesn't seem bothered by the uncertainty. He doesn't seem bothered by anything here.

"I'll call you when I get out." He smiles.

I nod quickly and turn away, trying the handle on the door too soon. The nurse buzzes it open again, and I leave. I walk fast as I escape down the hall and out the elevator. Even as I pass through the automatic front doors and across the parking lot, I can't ease my pace. It feels like there's someone chasing behind me. I jump in my car and lock both doors. I start up the engine and drive away from the hospital, knowing this time, I won't be back.

Chapter Thirty-One

The dirt lot comes up too fast. I have to pull over into someone's driveway to turn around. Once parked by the trailhead, I hurry into the woods with my backpack strapped on, anxious to get inside and hide my smiling face. Even though I'm away from the hospital and away from Steve, I still don't know how I feel. The miles of brush and trees conceal me from the outside world, but they don't do anything to stop the judgments raging inside.

My memories from being with Steve the last two days feel like a drug. I'm ruminating, I know, but something keeps pulling me back to replay the scenes over and over again. I hate this obsession. I shouldn't be smiling. I shouldn't be thinking about him in a romantic way, but I am. I'm not "just his friend" even though I keep insisting upon it. My counselor was right all along. I *do* have feelings for him. I always have. I was just afraid, and now I'm even more fearful of these feelings because they have reemerged at the worst possible time. *What's wrong with me?* I shouldn't be feeling this happy. I should be worried and sad, but *he* seemed so happy yesterday. *He's* the one who told the story of how we first met right before my hospital experience as if this was all some kind of fucked-up, cyclical love story. Not that I wasn't already thinking it. I was. Of course I was. How could I not? The story is obvious. As soon as he laid it out for the other patients, their eyes lit up like children in a movie theater. But do I believe it? Do I really love Steve or do I love being the counselor? Does he love me or does he love the darkness inside of me? Or an idea of me? Or am I completely off, completely delusional. In actuality, am I the only one in this equation asking any of these questions? I can't figure it out. I have to keep looping back.

Over and over again, I'm drawn to the warm memories—the ones that support my taboo feelings. In the hospital's kitchen area, I'm seated again next to Steve before all the other patients came around to gawk. I'm at the head of the table, and Steve's beside me on the corner, our knees almost touching. I can barely stay within the memory because the setting and my feelings are so messed up. The hospital is full of pain—it's still a nightmare to me—but it also holds sweet memories now. I shouldn't want to go back there, and I shouldn't be focused on love when I'm supposed to be a friend, but then Steve laughs at something I say and leans in close. Safe within the walls of the trees and the confines of my mind, I let go of the restraint from yesterday and seep into his gaze. I allow myself to feel attracted, feel comforted, and feel safe in his presence. I allow myself to think, not only about the last two days with him, but also about all last year. Every memory he and I ever shared together suddenly floods back up through a hole in the ground, soaking my feet.

I look down at my shoes. They truly are soaked. The entire trail is spotted with puddles, and I'm only just noticing. I step out from the center of the puddle and continue along the muddy edge. My rocks seem to weigh nothing as I balance my way around the shadowy pools. It's hard to believe this is the same path that frustrated me only a week ago—it looks so different. The trail turns a corner and takes me over a series of wooden bridges, lifting me several inches off the ground. This part I recognize. I speed up again, anxious to get to my destination. My boots touch the wooden planks, but in my mind, I am floating. I am lost in my reckless thoughts, spinning around like a carnival swing high in the air, orbiting the same idea, two taut chains connecting me to the center. I know I should try to come down, but I'm not sure if I want this ride to stop. The anger, suspicion, paranoia, and sadness still lingers, but mostly, I feel high. I walk my fingers up the metal links in my mind and gaze beyond my outstretched arm to the base. I see Steve. Every memory attached to him, once feared and buried, now swirls around freely. I can't decide how I feel about this. I need to get to the lake. I need another sign.

I hurry left down the pine-bedded path. The soft needles absorb every push of my rubber soles, slowing my pace slightly—enough to remind myself to breathe. A laugh bubbles up suddenly and bursts from my lips. I don't bother turning around to make sure I'm still alone. I know I look insane. Steve laughs too in my mind, the way he did yesterday with his head back, emotions unbridled. Maybe he was right all along. Maybe he and I are a perfect fit. I press my lips together and swallow. The anger whips through me again. *He stole my nightmare. He blurted it out carelessly for everyone to hear.* The emotions clash, confusing me. I don't know what I believe. I follow the path straight to the opening in the trees, where I hope to find some truth.

A gust of wind pushes me out from the path toward the water. Immediately, I am blinded. I squeeze my eyes shut and turn away from the lake, my hand up as a shield. Carefully, I squint to look again. To the left of the lake, the sun sits low in the sky, touching the water and setting the entire surface on fire. My eyes burn as I try to take in the beauty. I want to move closer—I've come all this way—but the light is too intense. I stand for a moment, not sure what to do, watching tiny neon worms drift across my glowing, eyes-shut world. Tears seep through the cracks of my lids, wetting my lashes. The beauty is undeniable in this bright sightless realm and the visions spectacular, but I know none of it is real. I turn around quickly to walk away.

As I reenter the woods, the trail seems darker. I walk carefully, eyes strained, trying to see through the smoke. Gradually, my vision adjusts, and the path becomes clear—the dimness was only temporary. All around me, the leaves flutter, crisp flakes of amber and red as delicate as flecks of ash. *How did I not notice all these colors before?* I look up to the spaces in between and marvel at the paper embers in the sky. I breathe in deep, taking in the bittersweet taste of autumn—a flavor by now I know pretty well.

As I head back to the dirt lot, I don't feel high anymore, but I don't feel out of control either. The carnival ride has stopped spinning. I'm floating back down to the ground. The rocks on my back still feel light, and so does my mind, but in a serene way. I watch my emotions float around me, smiling at their presence and this new-found distance in between.

When I get back to my car, out of habit, I check my phone. I'm not surprised to find a voicemail from the hospital. Before playing the message, I turn down the volume and put the sound on speaker. I hold the phone arm's length away as Steve's voice spills out:

> Hello, Melissa! This is Steve. I just wanted to let you know that it sounds like I will be getting out tomorrow. My sister is coming to stay with me for a few days, so maybe if you have time, you could meet her. That would be cool. Okay. I think that's it. I hope you're having a good day, and I'll see you tomorrow! All right, bye.

His giggle sends waves of energy through the speaker. They gush and surge through me, but I wait them out as the message clicks to an end. The energy fades as the silence ensues.

He is safe. He has his sister now, and he's going to be okay.

Without calling back, I put my phone in my purse and start up my car. As I drive home, I look around, my mind peaceful and open, taking in everything. The gradient hues of bruised sky and lavender clouds deepen above me. A woman standing on her front porch exhales cigarette smoke, a vacant look in her eyes. A pedestrian-crossing sign turned sideways drifts by, depicting an alternate world where people stroll straight into the ground. I smile gently as I observe these things. I don't remember seeing anything on the drive up here. Locked inside my head, possessed by my feelings, I was blind. I can't go back to being that way. I know too much.

As I drive over the Pell Bridge, I gaze past the cables' twinkling lights, back toward the trail from where I came. The last spark of sun slips beneath the trees, but I'm not sad. With my eyes wide open again, there is so much more that I'm able to see.

Chapter Thirty-Two

My tea is too hot, but I try to sip it anyway. Outside, the world is dark. The rain sprinkles down, a million droplets cling and slip down the window beside me. In the bright light of this coffee shop, I feel exposed. I look down at the rock in my lap, flipping it over to brush off some dirt and then turning it back around to stare at the painting on the front. I look too eager. I place the rock in the middle of the table instead and reach for my tea as I wait for Laura.

"Hey, sorry I'm late."

She slides off her dripping-wet jacket and hangs it on the back of the chair as I stand up to hug her.

"That's okay! I'm so happy you're here. I have something crazy to show you."

Her gentle eyes watch as we both sit down. I bump the table and shift in my seat as she settles in, lacing her fingers together. She waits for me to speak, but I don't know where to begin. I feel frazzled, aware of our mismatched states but still elated by my recent find. I glance again at the rock on the table. Her gaze follows.

"What is it?"

I take a quick breath, and then I blurt out everything in one long, pauseless sentence. By the end, I'm not even sure what I said. I had the whole story lined up in my head just a second before she arrived. I was ready to tell her each part in order: Steve's dinner invite from this morning, my pride in refusing, and of course, the magical hike where I found the daisy-painted rock. The story was perfect—polished and rehearsed internally—but as the words hit the air, they all seem to explode. My excitement compromises everything.

"Wait." She picks up the rock. "So you found this in the woods today?"

"Yes!" At least some of my words made sense. "Isn't that crazy? Someone painted it and left it there, just like what I've been doing all summer. I definitely think it's a sign!"

As she looks the rock over, I pull out my phone to open one of the articles I saved about daisies. I don't know how to frame this part of the story, so I read the Roman myth word for word. As I speak, I can't help adding in my own parentheses, relating Steve to Vertumnus and myself to Belides. I laugh, knowing I sound ridiculous but, at the same time, hoping I don't. As I reach the end of the myth—the part where Belides survives Vertumnus by turning herself into a daisy—I click the side button on my phone and let the screen go black prematurely. The end was supposed to be the best part—the most exciting and profound—but now I'm not so sure. I zipper my phone back up in my purse, my eyes averted. Laura returns the rock to the table without a sound.

"It's just a story." My laughter is strange. "There were other meanings too."

I peek up at Laura, surprised to find that she's still listening. I breathe in slowly, trying to absorb some of her calm.

"What were the other meanings?"

I laugh again.

"True love. That was actually the first one I found, but I'm definitely not going with that one."

She laughs too, a well of her own messy associations bubbling up. I'm relieved to have found a similar page. I take the cover off the top of my tea to let the steam pour out into the air, and then I ask her about her day.

"It was okay." She sighs. "To be honest, I really didn't feel like coming to our chakra class tonight. If we weren't doing this together, I probably would have skipped and stayed home."

"I felt like that last week." My eyes drift to the left, but I pull them back and smile. "It's funny, even though we basically just sit and close our eyes during these classes, it feels like a lot of work."

"Exactly! We go so deep every time. It's internal work." Her hands shoot up suddenly, her fingers rigid and her head bowed in between. "And so many people *aren't* doing their inner work. It drives me insane!" A laugh bursts from her lips, and then she shakes her head. "This is going to sound so smug, but sometimes I feel like I'm on a different level than other people."

"Like a different plane?"

"Yes!" We both lean back and laugh.

"So smug." I ease down. "But I get it. It's taken me a long time to step back and realize some of my patterns, and now that I know them, it's hard not to see them in others." I pause to breathe in. "I have faith though that most people want to change and grow too."

Laura looks to her right. I place a hand on her shoulder to bring her back.

"It's crazy." My voice is soft. "Some of the deepest, most introspective people I've met in this world have been diagnosed mentally ill."

"Mhm." She nods. The ripples are gentle, but the pull from the undercurrent is powerful. "What was that description you used for people like us? Something a friend told you a while ago?"

I smile because I could never forget the words. "'We feel deeper than most.'"

We both nod, breathing in slowly as we watch the steam from my tea. It continues to rise like a dancing curtain from the open cup. A constant, ever-changing wave.

"It's never gonna cool down." I laugh.

"It'll probably be perfect though by the end of class." She squints her eyes, both of us hypnotized by the steam. "Which chakra are we working on again today?"

"The throat."

"Mmm, the one about truth."

We nod our heads slowly again. The rain begins to pour outside, shifting our attention. We return to the topic of her day, discussing the underlying details beneath the mundane until we realize we only have a minute or two to get to class. She follows me separately down the road and parks beside me in the lot. I look to her through my wet window, eyes wide, gritting my teeth, and then we both bust out of our cars, laughing together as we rush through the rain. Once inside the building, we settle ourselves before entering the room. We wipe the rain and mirth from our cheeks and then quietly open the door to sit down on our adjacent mats. To our relief, we're not the last to arrive. The instructor holds off as we wait for the final two mats to be filled.

"You know what I realized on the way over here?"

Laura turns. "What?"

"The painting on that rock—sorry to keep bringing up that damn rock." We both laugh, struggling to contain ourselves. I feel like a kid trapped in school with the giggles again. "Okay, but seriously, I've been thinking. I realized the flower on that rock isn't really a daisy. It doesn't have enough petals."

"I noticed that too! What do you think it means?"

"I don't know." I turn away. "But I kind of prefer the spaces in between."

The door behind us creaks open as the last two people enter the room. They settle onto their mats as Laura and I turn back toward the center of the room. The instructor sits silently, cross-legged on her own mat with the rest of the class spread out like fingers all around her. We all close our eyes as she begins to speak, seeping into our own personal journeys yet held together by the same guiding voice.

Chapter Thirty-Three

At the bottom of the hill just before the tunnel of pines, I stop and turn, smiling at the rushing water. I must have taken a different path by mistake. By now, I thought I would know this trail by heart, but these woods continue to surprise me. I breathe in and close my eyes, listening to the falls. The water gushes and churns down the slope of clustered rock, a never-ending sound stirring up debris but also carrying it away. *A feeder.* My mom taught me that word. I hug in the straps of my backpack and sigh, turning back to the trail. I head up the hill.

On the edge of the pines, in an opening further down than usual, I find a map nailed to a roofed, wooden structure. I hold on to the frame and think of my dad. The sanded beams run like trunks beneath the bed of needles, deep and unseen underneath the packed earth. When I shake the frame, the cedar only budges slightly. I touch the dirt, wondering how far down the wood goes.

Along the map, I trace the trail. I run my finger over the smooth, laminated surface, following the yellow line. At the wide body of blue, I stop and lean in.

"No way. It's a river?"

I shake my head and continue on, drifting off the path to the small, familiar beach along the water. I unclip my backpack, leaning it against the tree, and sit with my legs dangling over the stone wall. The water laps gently up the sand, but further out, through squinted lids and different eyes, the middle does seem to move with a current.

I look up slightly to watch the last frays of sunlight slip beneath the distant trees. The sky deepens dark blue, mirrored in the water as rich sapphire. The two worlds reflect each other—one infinitely wide and untouchable, the other cold and contained. I've known both worlds. I've flown high above the clouds, soared months on imagined wings and faulty feathers, believing myself to be an eagle, a dragon, a superhero all in one. But I've also sunk deep down into the wet realm. I've ventured beyond where the fish swim into the muck where all living things disappear. I stare for a while at both blues, knowing neither world is sustainable. I can't survive long in either place because my wings are metaphors and so are my gills. The truth is I am human, and I've always been a bit lost, trying to squeeze my way into the black dividing line—the perimeter of trees where the sky and river meet, and the mysterious thread where the ocean and universe blur.

The precious hue darkens. I pull up my feet and cross my legs as the dull blue reaches up the sand. Underneath that water, when I was twenty-one, I didn't truly want to die. I thought I did—I thought that was the only way to reach the space between the muck and the clouds, but as I look now, imagining myself somewhere across the river in the black trees, I realize I'm already where I've always wanted to be. Just like the vision I had of myself on the lifeguard chair, the mirrored me in the trees doesn't smile. She gazes knowingly, the same way I gaze back at her from this side. Perspective in the moment is a difficult thing to master, but I think I'm finally starting to understand. For the first time in my life, I'm not yearning for the past or running scared toward the future. The thirteen-year-old girl no longer feels trapped inside, hiding with her head down within that cavernous space. My neck is strong as I gaze around, taking in the bigger picture.

My backpack tips over behind me, lopsided against the exposed root of the tree. I sigh. I'm not done healing. Inside the lumpy lining, there are still eleven rocks. I have no idea how long this project will take, but as I sit within the dark edge, a smile melts in. I don't care about time. I don't care if I ever finish. In this moment, I feel at peace. On the border of the sky and the water, I am in the middle of everything: the middle of seeing out my dreams and the middle of understanding myself; the middle of balancing my moods, loving my friends wholeheartedly, and enjoying my job; the middle of growing closer to my mom while at the same time growing away from my sister—not forever but for a period of time, opening up space for us to breathe, space for us to become our own separate trees. I'm in the middle of feeling both brave and afraid, supported and alone. I am in the middle of knowing all there is to know about love and knowing absolutely nothing at all. I am at the heart of my life—the center of healing, the center of it all.

Most people I know look back on the best years of their life, but right now, I'm looking around. Somewhere between the sun and the liquid surface, the moon and the cold wet floor, you'll find me. I hope to always exist here. I hope no matter what life brings that I will always be able to find my way back, somewhere in the middle.

Healing people heal people.

About the Author

Melissa Toni does not give up. When life knocks her down, she gets stronger. She is a lover of nature, an optimist of people. She believes healing is a process and a cycle—one that never ends.

CPSIA information can be obtained
at www.ICGtesting.com
Printed in the USA
LVHW031115051221
705331LV00003B/353